LITIGATING RELIGIONS

LITIGATING RELIGIONS

An Essay on Human Rights, Courts, and Beliefs

By

CHRISTOPHER McCRUDDEN FBA

The Alberico Gentili Lectures, 2015

OXFORD
UNIVERSITY PRESS

OXFORD
UNIVERSITY PRESS

Great Clarendon Street, Oxford, OX2 6DP,
United Kingdom

Oxford University Press is a department of the University of Oxford.
It furthers the University's objective of excellence in research, scholarship,
and education by publishing worldwide. Oxford is a registered trade mark of
Oxford University Press in the UK and in certain other countries

First Edition published in 2018

Published in the United States of America by Oxford University Press
198 Madison Avenue, New York, NY 10016, United States of America

British Library Cataloguing in Publication Data
Data available

Library of Congress Control Number: 2017958194

ISBN 978–0–19–875904–1

This essay is dedicated to my children, Joseph and Kathleen, with love, gratitude, and admiration.

PREFACE

This essay is a revised version of the Alberico Gentili Lectures I presented at the University of Macerata, Italy, in April 2015. I was deeply honoured to have been invited to give these lectures, as it enabled me to speak at one of the finest universities in Italy. But it was also somewhat intimidating, given the previous illustrious lecturers in this series. The first Alberico Gentili lecturer, in 2012, was Guido Calabresi, former dean of the Yale Law School, and my former professor at Yale. The second lecturer, in 2013, was Robert A. Burt, also Professor of Law at Yale Law School. The third lecturer, in 2014, was Giuliano Amato, now a distinguished judge of the Italian Constitutional Court. These were tough acts to follow!

The lectures are named after Alberico Gentili, the Italian jurist and Protestant dissident who, in the late sixteenth century, left Italy with his family to escape from the religious persecution he had suffered, eventually ending up as Regius Professor of Civil Law at Oxford. There, he became one of the first European scholars in public international law, practised law in London at the High Court of Admiralty, and became an honorary member of Gray's Inn, of which I am also a member.

When I was invited to give these lectures, I thought long and hard about the appropriate topic. Eventually, the answer was obvious: what better way to honour Gentili, recognize his religious persecution, celebrate his importance in the development of international law as an academic subject, and emulate his role as a legal practitioner who brings his cases into academic discourse, than to lecture on the relationship between human rights, religion, and litigation, drawing on my own experiences in court. I hope he would have appreciated the topic, and the method, if not my substantive argument.

★★★

My ambition in this essay is to present an accessible discussion, for a non-specialist audience, of some key themes and problems that arise in the courts when religions and religious beliefs enter the frame. It is not a textbook, or a monograph, in which you, the reader, will find a comprehensive account of the relationship between law and religion—there are already many such books available. Rather, I present here an interpretation of the phenomenon I describe as 'religious litigation' (to be defined in more detail subsequently). It is an attempt to make sense of the current puzzling and troublesome relationship between courts and religions.

In discussing these issues, I frequently draw on the vexed relationship between the Catholic Church and sections of the human rights movement. This is for several reasons. First, the Catholic Church is one of the biggest religions in the world, comprising (in 2017) well over one billion people, representing over 17 per cent of the world population, and is an important force globally. Second, the Catholic Church has a structure of hierarchically organized authority, with the Pope at the apex, which means that the Church's position on human rights is often more accessible than that of other churches. Third, as someone brought up in the Catholic tradition, I am more familiar with this religious tradition than with others, but I write from the perspective of a human rights academic and practitioner, not a theologian or a philosopher. Nor do I suggest that examples taken from this context are representative of engagement with human rights by other religions; they are merely illustrative.

It may be helpful at this point to summarize the basic argument that I make in the following pages. After setting out some examples of relatively recent cases in which conflicts between religious arguments and human rights arguments are identifiable, I ask why such tensions and conflicts have arisen between organized religions and the human rights system, and why so many of them land up in courts. I suggest that there are both ideological and institutional reasons for the phenomenon.

Three ideological developments are of particular importance. First, there have been significant developments in human rights doctrine that have resulted in religious practices coming more into conflict with human rights; second, there have been significant doctrinal developments within particular religions that have resulted in more fundamentalist approaches to doctrine being adopted; and, third, religious issues have increasingly become of renewed geopolitical significance, in some ways replacing, in other ways exacerbating, other ideological tensions. When these 'ideological factors' are set in a political context of significant migrations between countries of one religion and countries of another religion (or none), the stage is set for increased tensions and conflicts, including conflicts between religions and human rights.

There are also several institutional reasons why the courts have seemed an attractive forum in which these issues are now adjudicated. There have been institutional developments in human rights norm-setting and enforcement, and parallel changes in religions' organizational forms and political organization. I focus on the increased availability of courts to adjudicate disputes, on the developing role of NGOs in human rights litigation, on changes in religions' organizational forms and political organization, on the increased prevalence of domestic litigation and transnational religious litigation, and on intra-religious factionalism leading to judicial adjudication. All these factors play a role in helping to explain the phenomenon of religious litigation that I have identified.

Having attempted to account for the phenomenon of religious litigation, focusing on why these cases get to court, I then turn to consider what happens once these cases reach court. My argument is that in carrying out their adjudicatory task in these cases, there are three fundamental problems that the courts I discuss are faced with on a recurring basis. As a shorthand way of describing them, I call them the 'teleological' problem, the 'epistemological' problem, and the 'ontological' problem. These problems are not restricted to the judicial adjudication of claims in the area of religion, but few other areas of litigation consistently involve all three problems, at such a high level of intensity. I analyse each of these problems, and consider what role law and legal institutions play in addressing them.

By the teleological problem, I mean the problem that the courts face of deciding what the primary human rights protections relating specifically to religion are *for*, what their aim or *telos* is. There are two main sources of protection that, taken together, are the subject of the teleological problem: freedom of religion provisions, and freedom from religious discrimination provisions.

Although both are now common, there is essentially no consensus as to what they aim to achieve.

By the epistemological problem, perhaps using the term in a somewhat broader sense than some philosophers do, I mean the problem of how we are to understand normative systems other than those to which we ourselves are committed. By a 'normative system', I mean a system of belief that aims to say how we should act—normative systems are those where issues of 'ought', 'duty', and 'obligations' arise. Organized religions and human rights law are normative systems in this sense. The problem is how those involved in one normative system, say judges in interpreting human rights law, can understand another normative system, say Judaism, sufficiently well to be able to adjudicate on the meaning of that religion when conflicts arise that depend on an understanding of that normative system.

When I refer to the ontological problem, I am using the term 'ontological' in the specific context of what it means to be human, rather than in the sense of what it means to understand everything in relation to everything else. The ontological problem, understood as the problem of what it means to be human, arises in two particular respects in religious litigation. The first is the need to give content to the 'human' in 'human rights', and we see religions and legal interpretation giving diverse, and sometimes conflicting, answers to this question. One of the most contested sites of this conflict concerns how we are to understand the idea of 'human dignity', which is seen by several religions and by the human rights system as a foundational concept for the understanding of human rights.

The second respect in which the ontological problem arises has to do with the relationship between what it means to be human and the role of religion, with several religions viewing religion as central to our view of what it means to be human, and therefore conceiving protections for religion as central to the human rights enterprise. In the human rights law context, however, there appears to be increasing scepticism of whether religion should be part of human rights protections at all, and certainly whether it should be seen as, in any real sense, central to human rights.

If you have stayed with me to this point in the essay, I shall hope to have persuaded you of several key points. First, the relationship between human rights and religion in the judicial context is complex, changing, and problematic. Second, the relationship between human rights and religion is becoming more conflictual for reasons having to do with the changing role of religion, and the changing role of human rights. Third, the courts are intimately involved in adjudicating these conflicts, due to the changing institutional opportunity structure for litigation, both national and transnational. Fourth, although there is an overlapping human rights consensus between the main religions and human rights institutions, the current pattern of the relationship between human rights and religion is changing, and the hard-fought cases we will consider are not simply anomalies. Last, and most importantly, three particular and, I argue, central problems recur when courts have to deal with religious litigation: the teleological problem, the epistemological problem, and the ontological problem. Taken together, these problems exacerbate other tensions, bringing the courts themselves into the fray, preventing them from playing the role of standing above the conflict, and potentially threatening the human rights enterprise itself.

So, what is to be done? In Part III of the essay, I suggest that a revised approach is necessary, not just in how courts address issues in religious litigation, but more broadly in how we conceptualize human rights. I propose a reimagined understanding of human rights, building on the *practice* of human rights, which conceives human rights as providing the opportunity to consider fundamental aspects of what it means to be human, and the consequences this has for how we treat each other. The opportunity that human rights thus provides is one which offers the possibility of dialogue, but within constraints imposed by the overriding need that the dialogue should aim to further the human dignity of persons, rather than cut across it. The question I then pose is whether a true dialogue between human rights and religion can take place, and how this can best be encouraged.

In other words, how should human rights be *practised*, if we are to take seriously the idea of a true dialogue between secular and religious understandings of human rights? In particular, as Michael Ignatieff suggests, how can we best 'stop thinking of human rights as trumps and begin thinking of them as a language that creates the basis for deliberation'? If we aim to engage in a genuine dialogue in human rights practice, what are the practical implications for the courts' role? Identifying strategies that enable a genuine dialogue to take place over precisely the most contested questions in human rights has implications for how dialogue is conceptualized and practised by the courts, and the academic community. I propose that changes in the approaches that courts take in religious litigation should be encouraged. In particular, I suggest that taking pluralism, secularity, and accommodation more seriously as guiding principles would be an important starting point for a sustained and more productive relationship between religion and human rights.

By close attention to the developments and problems arising in litigation, and by imaginative sympathy with the religious internal point of view, we should be able to make theoretical progress. But dialogue is not a one-way street, and the question that I end with is whether *organized religion* is capable of engaging in a true dialogue, and what changes in approach from religious actors would help to secure such a dialogue. I suggest in particular that organized religion should be more conscious that external, human rights-based critiques of religion and of religious practices are potentially valuable to organized religion, and that an understanding of religious tradition supports just such a development. By the end, then, I suggest that despite the apparently irreconcilable differences between religion and human rights on display in much religious litigation, a more optimistic scenario is possible, in which a genuine dialogue takes place, one which is mutually beneficial.

***

This interpretation is necessarily affected by my own background and experiences. I grew up in Belfast, Northern Ireland, in the 1950s and 1960s. I was educated in Catholic schools and then read law at Queen's University Belfast during the period that saw the emergence of the civil rights movement. This movement sought to tackle religious discrimination in Northern Ireland, in part by relying on international and European human rights standards. By the early 1970s, however, Northern Ireland had descended into intercommunal violence and terrorism, which provided the ever-present backdrop to my undergraduate legal studies.

On graduating from Queen's in 1974, I then went to Yale Law School for two years of graduate work, supported by a Harkness fellowship, before undertaking a doctorate at Oxford University. By then, I had decided on an academic career, subsequently becoming a fellow and tutor in law at Lincoln College, Oxford and later Professor of Human Rights Law at the University of Oxford. I remained in Oxford until 2011, when I returned to Northern Ireland, and to Queen's, to take up a professorship of human rights and equality, my current position. Although primarily based in the United Kingdom, I have retained close links with the United States, and have taught regularly at the University of Michigan Law School since the late 1990s, subsequently becoming William W. Cook Global Professor of Law.

By the mid-2000s, I decided that I wanted to deepen my understanding of the ways in which law addresses human rights questions, by qualifying as a practising barrister, undertaking my practical training at Blackstone Chambers in London, which I subsequently joined as a member, and from which I currently practise. In that context, largely by accident it must be said, I was fortunate to be instructed as junior counsel in several of the most interesting cases in the United Kingdom concerning human rights and religion over the past few years (including the *JFS*, *Jivraj*, *Ladele*, and *Ashers Bakery* cases which I use as recurring examples). These have profoundly shaped my interpretation of the relationship between human rights and religious issues, as did my experiences in acting as legal adviser to the Catholic Bishops Conference of England and Wales during the passage of the same-sex marriage legislation by the UK Parliament (2012–13).

***

Professor Benedetta Barbisan of the University of Macerata was responsible for organizing these lectures and was a more gracious and welcoming host to my wife Caroline and myself than anyone has a right to expect. The rector of the University of Macerata, Luigi Lacchè did me the honour of introducing me, and I am deeply grateful to them both for making our stay in Macerata so enjoyable and interesting. I profited considerably from the discussions with those who attended the lectures. The original lectures and the discussions after each are available to watch on YouTube.

The first lecture may be accessed at: https://www.youtube.com/watch?v=akoYQ-NXYCM; the second lecture at: https://www.youtube.com/watch?v=-NYon76_Fdw; and the third lecture at: https://www.youtube.com/watch?v=UGpivE3djmQ.

The issues I discuss are situated in a fast-moving political and legal context, and I have incorporated developments since the lectures were presented, while retaining the overall structure, argument, and more relaxed tone of the lectures as presented originally, compared with the usual scholarly approach. In particular, I have eschewed the usual approach to providing references and citations. Instead of using footnotes or endnotes, viewing them as likely to be off-putting to non-specialists, I have experimented by providing a bibliographical essay at the end of the essay. I hope this approach will encourage a wider readership.

The lectures were written and presented while I was a fellow at the Wissenschaftskolleg zu Berlin (Berlin Institute for Advanced Studies, 2014–15). Wiko provided an ideal working environment, and I can only hope that whatever merit this book has will be seen as a modest 'thank you' to my colleagues during that wonderful year in Berlin.

Belfast, January 2017

CONTENTS

PART I
CONTEXT

1

CONCEPTS AND CASES

It wasn't supposed to turn out this way. As societies modernize, we were told, they would lose the vestiges of public religion and ultimately become committed to secularism. Religion would continue to exist, but would become publicly marginalized—or, 'privatized'—and excluded from the public realm. Secularization was the term coined to capture this process.

The idea that modernization leads inevitably to secularization is clearly false. Several societies that have modernized have deepened, rather than ditched, their commitments to religious identification—Malaysia, for example. Societies in the West have also seen a growth in religious pluralism, where a plethora of new religious groups compete with each other and with older-established world religions. And religion has increasingly been deeply embedded in what has been described as the clash of civilizations. Instead of the expulsion of religion from the public space, there has been a resurgence of a type of religious sensibility that is exactly contrary to the predictions, one which seeks, as Jeffrey Haynes puts it, 'the generalized "return" of religion to the public realm', what he terms '[r]eligious *de*privatization'.

Theories of secularization were, however, correct in at least one major respect. The continuing role of religion in public life *does* give rise to tensions with key aspects of modernity, not least with some aspects of human rights. The tensions arising between resurgent religion and human rights cannot be considered a transitional issue. On the contrary, they are likely to increase and fester if not addressed. Religions are a problem for human rights, and human rights are a problem for religions. And both, separately and together, are problems for the courts. This book is an attempt to introduce an interpretation of how religion and human rights interrelate in the legal context, and how this relationship might be reconceived. The context for my argument is

Litigating Religions: An Essay on Human Rights, Courts, and Beliefs. Christopher McCrudden. Published 2018 by Oxford University Press.

the increasingly fraught area of judicial reasoning in human rights litigation involving religious arguments, what I shall term 'religious litigation'.

SOME INITIAL CONCEPTUAL CLARIFICATION

We are faced with four definitional issues that I need to clarify at this initial stage of the argument: what I mean by 'human rights'; what 'judicial reasoning' involves; the vexed question of what 'religion' encompasses; and the meaning of 'religious litigation'.

First, what do I mean by 'human rights'? One approach to the question is descriptive; the other is normative. A descriptive approach attempts to answer the question by describing, for example, how the term has come to be used, and how it may have changed over time. Lawyers often say that human rights are those rights designated as such by law, whether domestic or international law. So, to the question, what are human rights, one response is to say: look at the Universal Declaration of Human Rights, or look at the International Covenant on Civil and Political Rights.

There is now a significant overlapping consensus between legal systems as to the specific rights that are in play when we speak of human rights. Thus, most human rights texts include the right to life, the right not to be tortured, the right not to be sold into slavery, the right not to be discriminated against, the right to have a private life, the right to freedom of conscience and religion, the right to freedom of expression, the right to marry, the right to be given a fair trial, and so on. However, these texts are so open-ended, and drafted at such a high level of generality, that the really hard questions of what they mean in practice are not at all clearly addressed, and we must (either explicitly or implicitly) adopt a normative approach to the meaning of human rights in order to interpret them.

By a normative approach, I mean that there is some attempt by the interpreter to reason through to the position that a particular claim is a human rights claim, supported by a particular right included in a human rights text, from a prior normative position. In the seventeenth and eighteenth centuries, advocates of rights derived them from God, or from what was 'natural'. In our own day, there has been no shortage of claimed normative underpinnings of human rights. Some have argued that they derive from the concept of equal concern and respect, some from notions of distributive justice, and some from ideas of what is necessary to satisfy basic social needs. Increasingly, it seems, the idea of 'human dignity' has become at least part of the basic normative discourse of human rights, an issue to which I shall return.

Viewed in this way, human rights are not just *legal* norms. Human rights documents often incorporate concepts of justice, dignity, and autonomy, which then inform the interpretation of the relatively open-ended legal provisions. Philosophy and political theory, for example, have a significant effect on some human rights law interpretation (and in turn have been affected by it, but that is a separate story for another time). Human rights law, therefore, is only relatively autonomous, although the degree of openness to 'external' human rights discourse varies significantly between jurisdictions.

It would be a mistake to think that we now have anything close to a settled normative interpretation of human rights in the legal sphere. Indeed, in some ways, it is difficult to speak of *the* legal understanding of human rights, since there are several competing conceptions. There are significant ideological differences between courts in their understanding of human rights in general and their understanding of specific rights in particular. Comparative law scholarship consistently points to different meanings that are attributed to 'human rights' in different jurisdictions. (I include, under the rubric of 'human rights', domestic constitutional rights protections and equivalent rights guaranteed by statute.) There are, for example, considerable differences between approaches to the idea of human rights in judicial reasoning in the United States and Europe. These differences in judicial reasoning are clear, for example, in the areas of abortion, hate speech, capital punishment, positive obligations on the state, extraterritoriality, the ability of non-citizens to secure protection, and how to manage conflicts of rights, to mention just a few.

By 'judicial reasoning' in human rights cases, I mean the interpretation of human rights texts by judges. This is what courts do, and what they are supposed to do, but the process and its results remain highly controversial. All the courts we shall be considering (primarily those in Europe, North America, and the Commonwealth) share a central problem of how to secure and retain legitimacy when interpreting these highly indeterminate texts. The only way, ultimately, to secure this legitimacy is by persuading their audiences that what they are doing is exercising *legal* judgement, but each court wrestles with how best to persuade its audience that it is exercising legal judgement in the contentious areas of human rights, and each has developed different techniques for doing so. The problem of judicial legitimacy will not go away for any of these courts.

Another key term I shall be using is 'religion'. Sociologists of religion tell us that the phenomenon of religion is difficult to pin down, in part because it appears to have several different facets or dimensions. The difficulty in pinning the concept of religion down, combined with the inherently controversial nature of religion when it comes into contact with the public sphere, and the changing contours of these political controversies when courts address them, make this area a continuing topic in litigation and the object of intense scholarly controversy. In this essay, I shall be considering primarily the tensions between religions and human rights arising in the context of several of the main world religions whose 'religious' nature is unquestioned—the religions 'of the book', Islam, Christianity, and Judaism.

What are the different dimensions of religion that these religions have in common? The first dimension is that there is a set of *beliefs* held by a group of individuals, usually about issues of transcendent importance to believers. The second dimension, worth separating from the system of beliefs, is that a particular religion often promotes a set of *values* that, it is claimed, flow from the transcendent belief system. The third dimension is that this set of beliefs and values is manifested in some form of *practice*, sometimes in public, which brings together those who hold those beliefs. The fourth element is that these religions are *institutional* in some form or other, with a designated group with some degree of authority within that religion, which has responsibility for leading religious practices, and sometimes for ensuring an element of doctrinal orthodoxy. The fifth element is that religion often becomes, independent of belief, a social *status*, a badge of identity, similar in some ways to other forms of identity, such as ethnic or cultural identity.

Finally, the idea of 'religious litigation' is broadly conceived to include what in the United States would be termed 'free exercise' and 'establishment' issues (protected by the First Amendment to the US Constitution), and what in Europe involves clashing understandings of 'freedom of religion' (protected by Article 9 of the European Convention on Human Rights (ECHR)). But it will include also issues that would be considered 'equal protection' issues in the United States arising under the Fourteenth Amendment to the US Constitution, and anti-discrimination issues in Europe, where the claim is for protection against religious discrimination (often arising under Article 14 of the ECHR). My conception of religious litigation goes beyond these issues, however. It includes, third, litigation that significantly involves a dispute over other issues (such as abortion, or same-sex marriage) in which religiously influenced claims are primarily framed as arising from some other right (such as 'privacy', protected under Article 8 ECHR, and the Due Process Clause of the Fifth Amendment to the US Constitution, or 'freedom of speech', protected under Article 10 ECHR, and the First Amendment, or the right to education, protected by the First Protocol to the ECHR). In these cases, arguments are made (whether for or against the claim) that are particularly associated with religious positions, but framed as engaging rights other than freedom of religion and non-discrimination.

SOME CASES

Several cases, from the United Kingdom, the ECHR, and the United States, illustrate well some of the tensions between religious positions and secular understandings of human rights, and will form running examples when we have to get to grips with my central arguments, as well as being interesting in their own right. They help to illustrate the three categories of religious litigation sketched out in the previous paragraph. These summaries are largely descriptions of the case adapted from the relevant court's own summary of the case; they are not intended as interpretations of the case; interpretations and critiques will come later in the essay.

JFS *case*

In the *JFS* case, the United Kingdom Supreme Court held that the admissions policy of a Jewish faith school constituted unlawful racial discrimination because it used the Orthodox Jewish interpretation of who is Jewish as a criterion for determining admission to the school. The Jewish community in Britain has several 'branches', and the Orthodox branch is but one (albeit the largest) and these branches differ, among other things, on the interpretation of who is Jewish, and on who has the authority to decide. E (M's father) and M were both Masorti Jews, which is one of the more 'liberal' branches of Judaism. E was recognized as Jewish by the (Orthodox) Office of the Chief Rabbi (OCR) but M's mother was not. She was Italian and, originally, Catholic but had converted to Judaism under the auspices of a non-Orthodox synagogue. Her conversion was not recognized by the OCR.

M's application for admission to JFS was rejected as he did not satisfy the OCR requirement of being Jewish. According to the OCR, his mother was herself not Jewish by reason of matrilineal descent, nor had she converted according to Orthodox requirements. M was not, therefore, Jewish by reason of descent from a Jewish mother. M was not himself converted according to Orthodox principles; nor was he undertaking a course of conversion according to Orthodox principles. M was, however, recognized as Jewish by the Masorti community on the basis of the conversion of his mother. M considered himself to be Jewish.

All the parties to the case accepted that JFS had engaged in *religious* discrimination, but that it was not unlawful. The British Equality Act 2006 had, indeed, introduced a prohibition on religious discrimination in schools admissions, but that could not be the basis for the application for judicial review because JFS was designated as a Jewish faith school and therefore fell within an exception permitting religious discrimination in admissions incorporated in the 2006 Act.

The case was fought, instead, on the basis of whether the school's admissions policy, favouring those who were 'Jewish' as defined according to Orthodox precepts, was discriminatory on grounds of *ethnic origin*. The Race Relations Act 1976 provided that discrimination in schools admissions was prohibited if such discrimination was ethnic discrimination, and there was no exception provided for faith schools from this provision. The major legal issue involved the meaning of 'discrimination'. 'Discrimination' included both 'direct' discrimination, and 'indirect' discrimination on the grounds of ethnic origin. E challenged the admissions' policy of JFS as directly discriminating against M on grounds of his ethnic origins, and this was the central issue. Alternatively, E claimed that the policy was indirectly discriminatory. The United Kingdom Supreme Court, unusually sitting as a panel of nine justices, held by a majority that JFS had engaged in unlawful direct discrimination on grounds of his ethic origins.

Ladele *case*

In the *Ladele* case, the European Court of Human Rights (ECtHR) upheld the dismissal of a marriage commissioner who refused to officiate at same-sex civil partnerships. Lillian Ladele was a marriage registrar, with years of good service, employed by a local public authority (the London Borough of Islington). The law in the United Kingdom changed while she was in post to permit civil partnerships between same-sex couples. Ms Ladele had a sincere conscientious objection to performing civil partnership ceremonies, arising from her Christian faith. In spite of her protests, Ms Ladele was designated to register and perform civil partnership ceremonies by the local authority, contrary to her religious beliefs.

The local authority was under no obligation to designate Ms Ladele as a civil partnerships registrar. Nor was there any need for her to be designated in order for the local authority to provide the service of registering civil partnerships. Prior to designating her, the local authority was aware of Ms Ladele's religious conscientious objection but did not consult her on its decision to designate. When she objected to being compelled to form civil partnerships and repeated her religious conscientious objection, she was disciplined for gross misconduct, and ultimately resigned as a result of the treatment she received. The local authority gave no weight to her religious beliefs.

Ms Ladele brought a claim for religious discrimination, alleging a breach of Article 14, taken together with Article 9. The Fourth Section of the ECtHR gave the case priority and joined it with three other cases (*Eweida, Macfarlane*, and *Chaplin*). The cases were joined as 'test cases' to allow the Court to identify and apply the relevant principles across an area of jurisprudence. In January 2013, the Fourth Section of the Court held by 5 votes to 2 that there had been no violation of Article 14 taken in conjunction with Article 9 in respect of Ms Ladele. The Grand Chamber did not agree to allow an appeal to be submitted, and the decision of the Chamber was therefore confirmed.

Hobby Lobby *case*

In the *Hobby Lobby* case, decided by the US Supreme Court, we can see a rather different approach being taken. This case concerned whether regulations promulgated by the Department of Health and Human Services (HSS), requiring employers to provide their female employees with no-cost access to contraception, violated the US Religious Freedom Restoration Act of 1993 (RFRA). This prohibits the 'Government [from] substantially burden[ing] a person's exercise of religion even if the burden results from a rule of general applicability', unless the government 'demonstrates that application of the burden to the person ... is in furtherance of a compelling governmental interest; and ... is the least restrictive means of furthering that compelling governmental interest'.

The owners of three for-profit corporations held sincere Christian beliefs that life begins at conception and argued that it would violate their religion to facilitate access to contraceptive drugs or devices that operated after the point of conception. The Supreme Court held (by 5 to 4) that, as applied to closely held corporations, the HHS regulations imposing the contraceptive mandate violated RFRA. The Court held that HHS's contraceptive mandate substantially burdened the exercise of religion, and that even assuming that the interest in guaranteeing cost-free access to several challenged contraceptive methods was a compelling governmental interest, the government had failed to show that the contraceptive mandate was the least restrictive means of furthering that interest.

HHS's contraceptive mandate substantially burdened the exercise of religion because it required the employers involved to engage in conduct that seriously violated their sincere religious belief that life begins at conception. If they and their companies refused to provide contraceptive coverage, they faced severe economic consequences. Even if they dropped coverage altogether, they also faced severe financial penalties. The Court considered that the employers' beliefs raised a difficult and important question of religious and moral philosophy, namely, the circumstances under which it is immoral for a person to perform an act that is innocent in itself but that has the effect of enabling or facilitating the commission of an immoral act by another. It was not for the Court, it held, to say that the religious beliefs of the plaintiffs were mistaken or unreasonable.

The Court held that the government had failed to satisfy RFRA's least-restrictive-means standard because HHS had not shown that it lacked other means of achieving its desired goal without imposing a substantial burden on the exercise of religion. The government could itself have assumed the cost of providing the contraceptives to women unable to obtain coverage due to their employers' religious objections. Or it could have extended the accommodation that HHS had already established for religious *non-profit* organizations to for-profit employers with religious objections to the contraceptive mandate. Accommodation of these types would not impinge on the plaintiffs' religious beliefs that providing insurance coverage for the contraceptives at issue violated their religion, but that it would still serve HHS's stated interests.

Surayanda *case*

Contrast this case with *Surayanda* v. *The Welsh Ministers*. Surayanda was a Hindu community in Wales. The preservation of life was a fundamental tenet of their beliefs and the slaughter of any animal was a direct violation of their spiritual values. Unfortunately, following the increased incidence of bovine tuberculosis (BTB) among cattle in the area, Welsh ministers adopted a policy which included the slaughter of all cattle that tested positive for BTB. Surayanda's temple bullock tested positive and the community was ordered to slaughter the cow. The community believed that the slaughter of the bullock 'would be a particularly sacrilegious act. A serious desecration of the temple, and comparable, in the Community's view, to the killing of a human being.' It asked for its bullock to be exempted from the policy of automatic slaughter, arguing that the community's right of freedom to manifest their religion under Article 9 ECHR would otherwise be infringed. The Welsh ministers entered into a dialogue with Surayanda and took account of expert evidence but subsequently confirmed the requirement that the cow must be slaughtered.

At this point, the community applied for and obtained judicial review of that decision. The judge who first heard the case found that the government had failed adequately to assess the degree of actual risk posed by the bullock, so that a sufficient balancing exercise had not been carried out in order to determine whether the admitted interference with the community's rights was proportional and necessary. The Court of Appeal for England and Wales decided, however, that the government was entitled to order the bullock's slaughter. The interference with the community's freedom of religion was necessary in the light of the importance of the policy to agricultural industry, the high incidence of BTB, and the reasonable expectation of those operating enterprises in that industry. The order requiring the slaughter of the cow was lawful, notwithstanding that the community considered the killing of the cow was akin to killing a human.

Hosanna-Tabor *case*

This case, decided by the US Supreme Court in 2012, involved an employee of a small Lutheran school. Teachers at the school were of two types: 'called' teachers and 'lay' teachers. 'Called' teachers were regarded as having been called to their vocation by God. 'Called' teachers completed a course of theological study and were Lutheran. 'Lay' teachers, on the other hand, were not required to have undergone theological training or to be Lutheran. Lay and called teachers generally performed the same duties. Cheryl Perich was a 'called' teacher. In addition to teaching secular subjects, she taught a religion class, led her students in daily prayer and devotional exercises, and took her students to a weekly school-wide chapel service, as well as leading this service occasionally.

She developed narcolepsy and was granted disability leave, after which she wanted to return to work, a request that was refused by the school. During her continuing attempts to persuade the school to allow her to return, Ms Perich disclosed that she had spoken with a lawyer and intended to assert her legal rights. After further increasingly acrimonious exchanges, she was dismissed, ostensibly for 'insubordination and disruptive behaviour', as well as the damage she had done to her 'working relationship' with the school, by 'threatening to take legal action'.

The US Equal Employment Opportunity Commission sued on her behalf, claiming that she had actually been dismissed because of her disability, in violation of the Americans with Disabilities Act. The school argued that the suit was barred by the First Amendment because the claims concerned an employment relationship between a religious institution and one of its ministers, invoking a 'ministerial exception', created by several lower courts in earlier cases. The Supreme Court agreed with the school, holding that the First Amendment did indeed bar litigation brought on behalf of ministers against their churches, claiming that their dismissal was in violation of employment discrimination laws. Requiring a church to accept or retain an unwanted minister, or punishing a church for failing to do so, intruded upon more than a mere employment decision. Such action interfered with the internal governance of the church, depriving the church of control over the selection of those who would personify its beliefs.

The Court held also that the exception covered Ms Perich, given all the circumstances of her employment. She was therefore barred from making an employment discrimination claim against the school. The lower court had held that the ministerial exception did not apply in the case, invoking a test focusing on the amount of time that the teacher spent in religious activities (which was quite small—leading daily prayer and worship, teaching religion classes; and taking her turn leading school devotions—most of her time was spent teaching mathematics). The Supreme Court disagreed, holding that determining who is and is not a minister is not, in principle, an activity that a stopwatch could answer, and that it was unprepared to second-guess the church's judgement in the case. She had a role distinct from that of most of its members. She had received a significant degree of religious training. Her job duties reflected a role in conveying the church's message and carrying out its mission. The purpose of the exception was not to safeguard a church's decision to dismiss a minister only when it is made for a religious reason. The exception instead ensured that the authority to select and control who will minister to the faithful was the church's alone.

Obst *case*

A different approach can be seen in two cases decided by the ECtHR, *Obst* v. *Germany* and *Schüth* v. *Germany*. These cases involved factually similar scenarios, but in decisions handed down on the same day in 2010 the Court appeared to reach opposite conclusions, both from *Hosanna-Tabor* and from each other.

The *Obst* case involved the dismissal by the Church of Jesus Christ of Latter-day Saints (often called the Mormons) of its director of public relations for Europe on grounds of adultery. Mr Obst had grown up in the Mormon faith and married in 1980 in accordance with Mormon rites. After holding various positions in the Mormon Church, he was appointed to his post in 1986. In December 1993, he confided to his pastor that he had been having an affair with another woman. The pastor advised him to tell his superior, which he did. A few days later, his superior dismissed him without notice for adultery. He contested the decision in the German labour courts and lost, whereupon he went to the ECtHR.

The Court examined whether the balance struck by the labour courts—between the right to respect for private life guaranteed by Article 8 and the rights enjoyed by the Mormon Church under Article 9 of the Convention which safeguarded the autonomy of religious communities against unjustified state interference—had afforded Mr Obst sufficient protection, holding that there was no violation of his rights. His dismissal amounted to a necessary measure aimed at preserving the church's credibility, having regard in particular to the nature of his post and the importance of the duty of absolute fidelity to one's spouse. The fact that the German courts had given more weight to the interests of the Mormon Church than to those of Mr Obst did not raise an issue under the Convention. Having grown up in the Mormon Church, he had—or should have—been aware, when signing the employment contract, of the importance of marital fidelity for his employer and of the incompatibility of his extramarital relationship with the increased duties of loyalty he had contracted towards the church as director for Europe of the public relations department. The duties of loyalty imposed on the applicant had been acceptable in that they had been aimed at preserving the credibility of the Mormon Church. The approach adopted by the German labour courts was not unreasonable.

Schüth *case*

The *Schüth* case concerned the dismissal of an organist and choirmaster in a Catholic parish church for adultery and bigamy. Mr Schüth's employment contract provided that the Code of Ecclesiastical Employment and Remuneration was an integral part of the contract. This Code had been adopted by several German Catholic dioceses and archdioceses. It required that the way of life of the employee and the members of his or her household should comply with the basic principles of the religious and moral precepts of the Catholic Church. A serious breach of these ecclesiastical principles was sufficient to justify terminating his or her contract without notice.

Eleven years after he began his employment, Mr Schüth separated from his wife, who was the mother of his two children, and began living with another woman, whom he subsequently married. The church dismissed him on the ground that he was in breach of the obligations of loyalty provided in the Code. The German Labour Court held that Mr Schüth's activity in his employment was in close proximity with the 'teaching function of the Church' and that the church's interest outweighed Mr Schüth's.

The ECtHR held, however, that the Labour Court had not examined whether Mr Schüth's employment was sufficiently close to the 'teaching function of the Church', and appeared simply to have followed the church's opinion on the matter. Since the case concerned a dismissal that occurred as a result of a decision by Mr Schüth relating to his private and family life, a more exhaustive assessment was necessary. The German court was required to balance the conflicting rights and interests involved, especially as Mr

Schüth's individual right to his private life was in opposition to the collective right to autonomy of the church authorities. There was insufficient explanation why the church's interests prevailed over Mr Schüth's.

Şahin *case*

Leyla Şahin, a practising Muslim, was a student at Istanbul University, and wished to wear a headscarf. After she began her studies there, a circular from the vice chancellor indicated that the wearing of headscarves was prohibited. She continued to wear her headscarf and was subsequently denied access to lectures and examinations. She unsuccessfully applied to have the circular set aside and disciplinary proceedings were brought against her. Ms Şahin subsequently left Istanbul to pursue her studies in Vienna and brought a complaint to the ECtHR. The Grand Chamber held that although there had been an interference with Ms Şahin's right to manifest her religious beliefs in preventing her from wearing headscarf, the interference with Ms Şahin's rights was justified in principle, proportionate, and necessary in a democratic society. The interference pursued the legitimate aim of protecting the rights and freedoms of others and protecting public order in a secular state. It was reasonable that universities would want to preserve the secular nature of the institution and restrict the wearing of religious attire. Article 9 was not an absolute guarantee of the right to behave in a manner governed by religious belief and it did not allow those who professed such beliefs to disregard rules that were justified, as in this case.

Lautsi *case*

Ms Lautsi, and her children, complained that the display of crucifixes in Italian state school classrooms violated their right to education under the ECHR and their right to freedom of thought, conscience, and religion. The school which the children attended had a crucifix on the wall in each classroom. Ms Lautsi protested, but the governors voted to keep the religious symbols as they were. The Italian Supreme Administrative Court, to which she complained, held that the presence of crucifixes in state school classrooms did not offend against the principle of the secular nature of the state.

The Grand Chamber of the ECtHR, which took up the case, reversed an earlier Chamber decision, and held that the mandatory display of crucifixes in the classroom of Italian state schools was within the bounds of the appropriate discretion allowed to states (the so-called 'margin of appreciation') and did not violate the right of parents to have their children educated in accordance with their religious and other views. The decision was particularly controversial in light of previous cases where the European Court had upheld state restrictions on the religious expression of *Muslims* in public schools, such as in the *Leyla Şahin* case. The Court in *Lautsi* considered that it was required to respect the state's decisions in matters of school curriculum and school management, including the place it accorded to religion, provided that those decisions did not lead to a form of indoctrination. A crucifix on a wall was an essentially passive symbol and could not be deemed to have an influence on pupils comparable to that of didactic speech or participation in religious activities, such as wearing a headscarf. There had been no violation of the right to education, and no separate issue arose under Article 9 ECHR.

Lawrence *case*

In *Lawrence* v. *Texas*, the Houston police, responding to a reported weapons disturbance in a private residence, entered Mr Lawrence's apartment and saw him and another adult man, Mr Garner, engaging in a private, consensual sexual act. Mr Lawrence and Mr Garner were arrested and convicted of 'deviate sexual intercourse' in violation of a Texas statute forbidding two persons of the same sex to engage in certain intimate sexual conduct. An earlier decision of the US Supreme Court had decided that such conduct was not protected, and that criminalizing the conduct was not unconstitutional.

In *Lawrence*, however, the US Supreme Court held that the Texas statute did violate the right of adults to engage in private conduct in the exercise of their liberty under the Due Process Clause, and overturned its own earlier decision. The Texas statute's prohibition touched on the most private human conduct, sexual behaviour, and in the most private of places, the home. The liberty protected by the Constitution allowed homosexuals the right to choose to enter upon relationships in the confines of their homes and their own private lives and still retain their dignity as free persons. The fact a state's governing majority has traditionally viewed a particular practice as immoral, influenced by their religious beliefs, was not a sufficient reason for upholding a law prohibiting the practice.

Obergefell *case*

In *Obergefell* v. *Hodges*, fourteen same-sex couples and two men whose same-sex partners had died claimed that the US states in which they lived were in violation of the Fourteenth Amendment by denying them the right to marry their same-sex partners. The state authorities, supported by a range of organized religions, argued that it would demean a timeless institution if marriage were extended to same-sex couples. The US Supreme Court held that the Fourteenth Amendment required a state to license a marriage between two people of the same sex and to recognize a marriage between two people of the same sex when their marriage was lawfully licensed and performed out of state.

The fundamental liberties protected by the Fourteenth Amendment's Due Process Clause extend to certain personal choices central to individual dignity and autonomy, including intimate choices defining personal identity and beliefs. Decisions about marriage are among the most intimate that an individual can make. Same-sex couples have the same right as opposite-sex couples to enjoy intimate association, a right extending beyond mere freedom from laws making same-sex intimacy a criminal offence, as was in issue in *Lawrence*. Without the recognition, stability, and predictability marriage offered, children suffered the stigma of knowing their families are somehow lesser. They also suffered the significant material costs of being raised by unmarried parents. The marriage laws in issue, held the Court, harmed and humiliated the children of same-sex couples. In addition, since marriage is a keystone of the United States' social order, it was demeaning to lock same-sex couples out of a central institution of the society. The limitation of marriage to opposite-sex couples may long have seemed natural and just, but its inconsistency with the central meaning of the fundamental right to marry is now manifest.

The right of same-sex couples to marry was also derived from the Fourteenth Amendment's guarantee of equal protection. The challenged laws burdened the liberty of same-sex couples, but they also abridged central precepts of equality. The marriage laws at issue were in essence unequal: same-sex couples were denied benefits afforded opposite-sex couples and were barred from exercising a fundamental right. Especially when set against a long history of disapproval of their relationships, this denial resulted in a grave and continuing harm, serving to disrespect and subordinate gays and lesbians.

2
IDEOLOGY

The cases that I described in the previous chapter have, I hope, whetted your appetite, although they may also have puzzled you. Aren't many of these cases going in different directions? Isn't there a significant amount of change in how similar issues are being considered over time? Don't different states appear to take inconsistent approaches despite operating on apparently similar principles? What difference, if any, does it make to the result of the case, if the religious issue is presented as engaging one human right or another different one? If the cases appear confusing to you, then that is because they are! My aim in the remainder of the essay is to try to make some greater sense of the phenomenon of religious litigation in the human rights context, of which these cases are merely the tip of the iceberg, to explain why this phenomenon has arisen, and what it says about current religious debates, and human rights more generally.

In this and the following chapter, we consider why these tensions and conflicts have arisen between organized religions and the human rights system, and why so many of them seem to land up in courts. In brief, there are both ideological and institutional reasons. In this chapter, I shall be primarily concerned with the ideological aspects and in the next chapter with the institutional aspects, although I recognize that this distinction will seem too stark for some.

Three ideological developments are of particular importance, and are discussed in the second part of this chapter. First, there have been significant developments in human rights doctrine that have resulted in religious practices coming more into conflict with human rights; second, there have been significant developments within particular religions that have resulted in more 'fundamentalist' approaches to religious doctrine being adopted; and, third, religious issues have increasingly become of renewed geopolitical

Litigating Religions: An Essay on Human Rights, Courts, and Beliefs. Christopher McCrudden. Published 2018 by Oxford University Press.

significance, in some ways replacing, in other ways exacerbating other ideological tensions. When these 'ideological factors' are set in a political context of significant migrations between countries of one religion and countries of another religion (or none), the stage is set for increased tensions and conflicts, including conflicts between religions and human rights.

Before considering these ideological changes, we need, first, to appreciate the basic human rights structure that often governs the relationship between the state and religion. In the first part of this chapter, therefore, I shall sketch out, in a preliminary way, the overlapping consensus that has emerged regarding how states now address religions legally, both in constitutions and in ordinary statutes. This consensus relates to the forms in which the discourse takes place, rather than on the application of these forms to particular conflicts. There is a second preliminary point of some importance. The degree of consensus surrounding the appropriate legal norms applying to the relationship between religion and human rights extends beyond law into the values that both systems adhere to. It would be misleading to ignore, or take for granted, the significant degree of convergence between religious teaching and the values that underpin secular human rights norms. Values such as liberty, equality, solidarity, autonomy, and dignity are shared, at least at a high level of generality, even if applied differently. We shall be considering instances where there has been tension and conflict between organized religions and human rights over the interpretation and application of these and other values, and we shall have much to say about these tensions, but we shall begin by making it clear that there is more of an overlapping ideological consensus than might be supposed if we were to focus only on the type of disputes we encountered in the first chapter.

DEVELOPING LEGAL APPROACHES

In identifying the overlapping consensus on how the law deals with religion in the jurisdictions we shall be considering, we can usefully begin with the United States. The influence of the United States in the development of the conceptual legal tools used to address the relationship between the state and religion has been exceptionally important in many jurisdictions. Essentially, it consists of three ideas: first, that the state should not unduly curtail the right of individuals to practise their religion; second, that the state should not itself adopt or embrace any particular religion or (more controversially) religion in general, in a way that elevates that religion or religion in general to other than a symbolically special position; and, third, that the state (and, in some circumstances, other private parties, such as employers) should not discriminate between religions or treat individuals less favourably on the basis of their religious beliefs.

More technically, and adopting the language of the US Constitution, we find protections for the 'free exercise' of religion (the first idea), counterbalanced by 'non-establishment' of religion (the second idea), found in the First Amendment. It is through these constitutional provisions that religious issues are primarily considered. The First Amendment has been regarded as incorporating an element of non-discrimination (the third idea), within the meaning of 'free exercise' and 'non-establishment'. As a result, the equal protection clause of the Fourteenth Amendment has rarely been called on to support a religious discrimination claim, because it has not been perceived as necessary, given the First Amendment.

At the US statutory level, the third idea (non-discrimination on grounds of religion) is developed further, in particular in Title VII of the federal Civil Rights Act 1964, which prohibits religious discrimination but only in the employment context. It is clear that the approach taken to the interpretation of Title VII in this respect is mostly dominated by the approach taken in the First Amendment. What is noteworthy about Title VII's approach to religion, however, is the requirement of 'reasonable accommodation', a concept with which Europeans are much more familiar in the context of disability discrimination. It means, essentially, that employers are under a (relatively weak) obligation to 'accommodate' the religious practices of their employees, where that is 'reasonable'. The relatively restrictive approach taken to the meaning of reasonable accommodation in US litigation has meant, however, that the 'reasonable accommodation' approach has really only taken off when it transmigrated into Canada, and was adopted by the Canadian Supreme Court in its interpretation of the freedom of religion provisions of both the provincial anti-discrimination statutes, and the Canadian Charter of Rights and Freedoms.

These three elements (free exercise, non-establishment, and non-discrimination) are also reflected, to a greater or lesser extent, in international and regional human rights treaties. These commonly incorporate a 'freedom of religion' protection (which is often interpreted as guaranteeing the freedom from being coerced into the practice of religion by the state). An 'anti-discrimination' provision also commonly guarantees the right not to be discriminated against by the state (sometimes only in particular situations) on a series of grounds, one of which is often 'religious belief'. Thus, for example, the European Convention on Human Rights (ECHR) protects 'freedom of religion' in Article 9 ECHR, and 'freedom from discrimination' on the basis of religious beliefs in the exercise of other Convention rights in Article 14 ECHR.

This tripartite set of provisions is now commonplace and several of the jurisdictions which we shall be considering have adopted this approach, such as Canada, the United Kingdom, and South Africa, influenced by developments in the United States and international law. We shall see, however, that in particular jurisdictions one or other of these three elements may be emphasized more than others. This can be seen in the way religion came to be protected in the development of European Union (EU) law. The approach taken is one that provides an anti-discrimination remedy, but (at least until the EU Charter of Fundamental Rights) did not attempt to guarantee freedom of religion as such. And the obligation on Member States to incorporate EU law into their national law has therefore meant that the anti-discrimination element in dealing with religious-secular relationships is now strongly present (at least formally) in EU Member State laws.

The way in which the law addresses religion in Britain illustrates well the influence of these transnational developments. Freedom of religion came into British law through the Human Rights Act 1998, which effectively incorporated the ECHR into British law. The prohibition of religious discrimination, on the other hand, has been heavily influenced by developments in *EU* law. The introduction of the 2000 EU Directive prohibiting employment discrimination based on religion (and other grounds) resulted in the introduction into UK law of an expanded anti-discrimination remedy. British anti-discrimination law was broadened beyond freedom from discrimination on grounds of race and ethnic origin, to encompass freedom from discrimination on grounds of religion, and this was in part justified because of the protection that this would bring to minority religious communities, such as Muslims, who were assumed to be outside the protection of the race discrimination prohibition.

The British Equality Act 2006 went further and expanded the coverage of religious discrimination prohibitions beyond employment. The later British Equality Act 2010 now proscribes discrimination on the basis of 'religion or belief' in several additional contexts, including the provision of goods and services, housing, and (to a limited extent) schools. 'Religion' is defined as meaning 'any religion and a reference to religion includes a reference to a lack of religion'; 'belief' means 'any religious or philosophical belief and a reference to belief includes a reference to a lack of belief'. The United Kingdom also adopted a set of provisions imposing additional obligations on public authorities to have 'due regard' to how 'equality of opportunity' (a broader concept than anti-discrimination) can be ensured by the public authorities. Since the 2010 Act, the grounds on which public authorities have to consider 'equality of opportunity' include religion.

This preliminary sketch of developments has suggested, I hope, the complexity of the legal and political landscape that we are about to enter. Although each jurisdiction is unique, there are several common themes that the developments illustrate. In particular, three central legal elements may be identified in the human rights protection of religion (the protection of freedom to practise religion, the protection of freedom from religion, and protection from religious discrimination).

OVERLAPPING CONSENSUS BETWEEN RELIGIONS AND HUMAN RIGHTS

Turning now to the second preliminary point: that although we shall often emphasize tensions between organized religion and human rights, there is also a significant overlap between the ideology of human rights and the ideology of several organized religions. The relationship between the Catholic Church and the human rights movement, for example, can legitimately be characterized as one of significant convergence, as well as one of tension and ambivalence.

The Catholic Church's position on constitutional rights and the 'Rights of Man' as they grew out of the Enlightenment and the French Revolution was initially hostile, and continued to be guarded for many years. The Church's Pontifical Commission Justice and Peace, in its remarkable statement *The Church and Human Rights* first published in 1975, and reissued in 2011, pointed out that: '[T]he Catholic Church's attitude towards human rights during the last two centuries too frequently has been characterized by hesitations, objections, reservations and, on occasion, even vehement reaction on the Catholic side to any declaration of human rights made from the standpoint of liberalism and laicism.'

The Popes since 1948 have, however, supported the Universal Declaration of Human Rights, if in rather guarded terms initially. In the 1960s, the role of Pope John XXIII was critical in providing a bridge between the post-Second World War human rights discourse and the *magisterium* (the teaching of the Church), culminating in *Pacem in Terris*, the papal encyclical that did more than any other single document to signal a rapprochement between Catholic teaching and human rights developments at that time. This was subsequently confirmed by the Second Vatican Council ('Vatican II') in *Gaudium et Spes* and *Dignitatis Humanae*.

It is hard to overestimate the importance of these texts. They mark a fundamental change of the Church's position on human rights, carried through in the Second Vatican Council and by subsequent Popes. In brief, and rather simplistically, before Pope John XXIII's encyclical, human rights were seen as too closely connected with those aspects of liberalism, modernity, and the Enlightenment that the Church opposed. *Pacem in Terris* marks the acceptance, indeed the embracing, of human rights discourse. Since then, Church authorities have stated that: '[I]nternationally accepted human rights standards are strongly supported by Catholic teaching'. The Holy See has also ratified several multilateral human rights treaties, and incorporated references to international human rights standards in Concordats (treaties) with several states. From various texts we can piece together a fairly comprehensive list of rights that the Church recognizes that substantially overlaps with any similar list that secular human rights lawyers would produce. In terms of substance, on torture, racism, the rights of the child, the need for basic levels of subsistence, and so on, there is a clear overlapping consensus at the level of principle. Indeed, there is also, thanks to Jacques Maritain, an overlap in the basic theory of why human rights are important: both the Church and international human rights rhetoric explain human rights in terms of the need to recognize human dignity.

During the 1960s, then, there was a significant opening up to human rights thinking. Why the Catholic Church was willing to adopt human rights thinking is still the subject of considerable historical investigation and interest, but in part it is likely that the human rights agenda was seen as having sufficient overlap with Church positions on issues of justice, welfare, and the common good to be worthy of support. The Church's decline as a secular power also resulted in greater self-awareness of the Church's moral voice in the world, a voice that could be articulated in the language of human rights, and the development of Catholic understandings of freedom of religion and conscience was partly articulated in human rights terms. It is also probable that the influential involvement of Catholics, such as Maritain, in discussions on the content of both the Universal Declaration of Human Rights and the ECHR in the late 1940s was seen as giving a seal of approval to the process, further underpinning the presumption that human rights would have little disruptive effect on Church doctrine and practice (not least because of the apparently strong protection for religious freedom within these human rights documents).

There may well be an additional reason. There is a general proposition about the diffusion of human rights standards that is now so well accepted as to be almost trite: stable democratic states that participate in the drafting of human rights documents do so primarily *pour encourager les autres*. That is, they expect that these norms will affect the behaviour of *others* rather than themselves. Another way of putting the same point is that human rights are often initially seen in foreign offices and state departments as primarily for export only, because most stable democratic states consider their own internal human rights positions to be relatively satisfactory; in need of tweaking, perhaps, but fundamentally in compliance with human rights obligations. It is often only much later that these states discover that human rights have a tendency to morph in such a way that leaves such states exposed to criticism of their own compliance. It would be surprising if similar motives were not also pervasive in the Vatican of the 1960s.

There are, I repeat, many common elements that constitute a substantial degree of overlapping consensus. Here are a few. The human rights tradition sees the state as subject to positive obligations to protect the right holder against others, whether they be state actors or not. The Catholic tradition is aligned with the human rights approach on this issue. There is a strong preference for a state whose duty it is to actively bring about the conditions under which rights are protected. In the terms we have just identified, there is a preference for positive obligations: 'It is ... demanded by the common good', says *Pacem in Terris*, 'that civil authorities should make earnest efforts to bring about a situation in which individual citizens can easily exercise their rights'.

Like several of the most progressive national constitutions, and international human rights law itself, the Church's position, again reflected in *Pacem in Terris*, is straightforward: strongly in favour of an approach to human rights that incorporates socio-economic rights. Indeed, in several respects, Catholic social teaching outstrips what lawyers would consider is currently required by human rights law. In this context, the Catholic 'preferential option for the poor' has important practical implications for how these rights are to be protected. 'Rights to be free from economic deprivation', writes Shupack when discussing the implications of the preferential option, 'take precedence over some traditional autonomy rights. For example, rights to private property and free commerce are subordinated to the right of subsistence with dignity.' He continues: 'Private property should be subject to the principle that it be used for the common good, thereby authorizing government to regulate, tax, and occasionally expropriate property on behalf of the poor.'

We should not, then, over-accentuate the tensions. In some particular respects, however, it is clear that religious and secular conceptions of human rights *have* diverged significantly, as we shall see subsequently. In these areas, human rights have become a central site of normative contestation over the implications of modernity, with both sides claiming to interpret human rights in the 'right' way. This is possible because of the contested nature of human rights standards, and their sources of authority, as well as confusion as to whether there is a lexical ordering of the importance of particular human rights compared with others. Both sides see themselves as proponents of human rights, often claiming different human rights, or different interpretations of the same right, in support of their positions.

So, despite a relatively strong overlapping consensus in how the relationship between religion and the state should be structured, and a degree of consensus on human rights, principles, and values between at least one major religion and human rights institutions, severe tensions are now evident, as can be seen by looking again at the cases described in the first chapter. Why did we get to this situation? The reasons have to do with changes in human rights doctrine, internal debates within the organized religions, the role of religion in geopolitical disputes, and the increased importance of migration. It is to these that I now turn in the second part of the chapter.

CHANGES IN HUMAN RIGHTS DOCTRINE

We now turn to consider the ideological changes that I have suggested contribute to tensions between human rights and organized religions, beginning with the significant changes and developments in human rights doctrine that have increased this tension, and opened up further opportunities for conflicts to arise. Two developments are of particular importance.

First, with the increasing emphasis on racial and gender equality from the 1960s onwards, morphing into a more general concern to enable individual identities to be valued and protected, equality discourse in the human rights context took on a strongly individualistic, autonomy-based, anti-essentialist, and constructivist rhetoric, one which was at odds with that adopted by several organized religions.

Of these, the anti-essentialist turn is the most interesting, in my view, especially when taken together with the constructivist approach. There are, of course, several different meanings that may be intended by the use of the term 'essentialist'. I use it here to refer to the idea that 'definitions are descriptions of the essential properties of things, and that one can evaluate attempts at definitions in terms of the falsity or truth of the descriptions given by them'. Essentialism is now most used in the social sciences as a description of a position that is regarded as outdated, a term of criticism rather than approbation. As Simon Blackburn explains, 'Essentialism is used in feminist writing of the view that females (or males) have an essential nature (e.g. nurturing and caring versus being aggressive and selfish), as opposed to differing by a variety of accidental or contingent features brought about by social forces.' Often such 'essentialism' is seen as based on biological determinism.

It is this understanding that anti-essentialism seeks to challenge, viewing roles as socially constructed and provisional. In particular, social *identities* are seen as socially constructed and changeable. Human rights discourse and, to a notable extent, human rights law, has significantly (but by no means uniformly) adopted an anti-essentialist understanding of, for example, gender equality and sexual orientation. In contrast, as we shall see subsequently, several organized religions (perhaps particularly Catholicism and Islam) have anthropological understandings of the relationship between women and men, and understandings of gender and sexual orientation more generally, that are strongly essentialist.

These are not the only significant changes in human rights doctrine that contribute to greater tensions between religion and human rights. A second development proved equally important. Broadly speaking, international human rights law used to have relatively little to say, either pro or con, about many issues which had a religious dimension. This distance resulted from several different elements of the then dominant interpretation of human rights: first, human rights primarily applied to actions by the state or state-sponsored bodies, not to non-state actors, such as many organized religions; second, human rights primarily imposed negative obligations on the state rather than positive obligations on the state to regulate others; third, human rights at least as enforced primarily related to the protection of civil and political rights, such as those found in the International Covenant on Civil and Political Rights, rather than those found in the International Covenant on Economic, Social and Cultural Rights (such as the right to health, where controversial issues around contraception and abortion often arose); and, fourth, there were 'private' areas such as sexual morality and intra-family relations that were regarded as inappropriate for international intervention and were considered firmly within the sphere of national sovereignty. The result was to leave large swathes of activity regarding women and sexual minorities, for example, unaddressed in international human rights discourse. Prior to the 1980s, international organizations, states, and NGOs interpreted 'human rights' as substantially inapplicable to many 'traditional' practices which particularly impacted women's lives. Perhaps the best-known such issue was that relating to female genital cutting, which was long off-limits as an issue of international human rights concern.

Since the 1980s, however, each of these elements in the dominant interpretation of human rights has been severely challenged: actions by non-state actors are increasingly seen, at least by NGOs, as included within the sphere of international human rights activism; positive obligations on states to ensure the adequate implementation of rights within their jurisdictions by all, including 'private' actors, have become commonplace in human rights discourse; socio-economic and cultural rights have attracted significantly greater enforcement attention than before; and international human rights actors now consider it legitimate for human rights norms to address issues in the 'private' sphere, and, indeed, to make them a central focus of their attention.

As a result of these changes in human rights practice, women's rights and the rights of marginalized sexual minorities increasingly came to dominate human rights discourse (at least in Western states and in international organizations). When these developments were combined with a noticeable reduction in the guilt that Western states felt over their former colonialism, 'traditional' religious practices came more into the firing line. Since then, there has been a persistent attempt by international and regional organizations with norm-creating human rights responsibilities to ensure that human rights standards trump conflicting 'traditional' practices in the global South, whether religious, cultural, or customary. This has resulted in a plethora of texts and interpretative statements, as well as national judicial practice, reflecting this position, such as the Human Rights Committee Resolutions on child marriages and forced marriages, in which 'traditional values' were seen as undermining human rights standards. One of the best-known illustrations of the changes that these doctrinal developments contributed to is that relating to how female genital cutting is regarded in human rights law. From being an issue that few were willing to identify as a breach of human rights standards, it is now widely so regarded.

DEBATES WITHIN ORGANIZED RELIGIONS

As well as changes in human rights doctrine, there have been significant shifts within organized religions, in some cases developing positions that are more antagonistic to some human rights development than previously. Developments within the Catholic Church again illustrate the point. We saw previously that by the early 1960s there was a growing rapprochement between the Church and the developing international human rights movement, culminating in *Pacem in Terris*. Since then, however, the Church has been engaged in an intense continuing debate about how best to respond to such secular developments in human rights. Bernard Lonergan's 1967 essay which considers the heated debates within the Catholic world at that time contrasts two modes of thinking about meaning, those characteristic of 'classical' and 'modern' culture, with the former being ahistorical and essentialist, secure in having clear and accepted meaning, while the latter is more historical and inductive. He viewed Catholic moral theology as born in the former and by the mid-1960s confronted with the latter world of meaning. Lonergan anticipated a split in Catholic theology in which 'a scattered left' develops 'captivated by now this, now that new development, exploring now this and now that new possibility' in contrast with 'a solid right that is determined to live in a world that no longer exists'.

John Langan, although using the terms 'revisionist' and 'anti-revisionist', has suggested something similar to me with 'revisionist' and 'anti-revisionist' being equivalent to Lonergan's 'modern' and 'classical' respectively. The main factors making for revisionism are: the importance of historical conscientiousness;

the general theological awareness of the *development* of doctrine; a desire for a more culturally and psychologically sensitive pastoral practice; and the social distance between ecclesial authority and the profession of theology. The main factors making for anti-revisionism are: an essentialist, legalistic, and biologistic conception of natural law as developed in neo-scholasticism, with a strong emphasis on its immutability and universality; the assertion of papal authority in moral matters since the mid eighteenth century (in the First Vatican Council), with a preoccupation on infallibility and the irreversibility of Church teaching.

A major intellectual development took root in the late 1960s that contributed to opening up the perceived gap between the human rights movement and the Catholic Church. From the early 1960s, there was a sustained attempt to rethink and reformulate the foundations of 'natural law' in a way that grew from and was consistent with Thomist approaches. One of the most influential of these attempts was what came to be called 'new natural law' by its proponents and opponents. 'New natural law', as articulated by a group around Germain Grisez, and including John Finnis and Robert George, became in practice a controversial challenge to revisionist approaches within the Church that were much more in tune with emerging human rights norms. 'New natural law' was seen by some elements of the Church hierarchy, particularly in the United States, as supportive of the traditional elements of some of the existing *magisterium* and in turn to be supported and encouraged, particularly after the bitter controversy that arose within the Church on the publication of *Humanae Vitae*, concerning contraception.

The major difference between revisionism and anti-revisionism lay in their differing anthropological understanding. The result is a sharp dispute, *within* the Church, over what is required to ensure human flourishing. Both approaches appeal to human dignity, but there is sharp disagreement as to what human dignity requires. Sometimes, a revisionist understanding of dignity is evident, particularly in the social teaching of the *magisterium*; sometimes an anti-revisionist approach to dignity, more compatible with new natural law, is evident, particularly in some of the teaching of the *magisterium* in areas touching on gender and sexual orientation. When anti-revisionism is dominant, the likelihood of tensions with human rights norms is increased.

There are several aspects of the Catholic conception of human rights that are out of sympathy with the current interpretations of human rights. As Zachary Calo has written, a 'distinctive [Catholic] understanding of rights theory' has evolved, one 'that has both incorporated the insights of liberalism while nevertheless remaining at tension with it in several fundamental respects'. The period of rapprochement between the two, evident during the papacy of John XXIII (reflected in *Pacem in Terris*), and the papacy of John Paul II (regarding the need for freedom and democracy in central and eastern Europe), now seems under severe challenge. The Church's approach to the role of women, issues of sexual orientation, contraception, abortion, genetic manipulation, and physician assisted suicide, to name but a few current issues, increasingly appear to conflict with emerging human rights norms in these areas.

The Church's official *practice* towards human rights also appears to manifest a deep unease. One example must suffice. The Holy See's record in ratifying human rights instruments is, to put it bluntly, abysmal, putting it somewhere on the level of Zimbabwe and Saudi Arabia in terms of the number of major human rights treaties not ratified, and just below the United States. The rhetoric of support for the Universal Declaration simply doesn't translate into willingness to be bound in international law. The Holy See has ratified the Convention on Race Discrimination, the Torture Convention, and the Convention on the Rights of the Child. But, as of January 2017, the Holy See had not ratified the International Covenant on Civil and Political Rights, the International Covenant on Economic, Social and Cultural Rights, the Convention on the Elimination of all Forms of Discrimination Against Women, or the Convention on the Rights of Disabled People. Many countries ratify these conventions while at the same time entering reservations on particular issues. This is also open to the Holy See. For the Holy See not to ratify these conventions at all cannot be justified simply on the basis that a particular provision causes difficulties; that would be a reason to enter a reservation. No, the signal sent by non-ratification is unease about these Convention as a whole, and to some extent at least, a desire to distance itself from aspects of the human rights system.

RELIGION AS A GEOPOLITICAL FOOTBALL

We see that there have been ideological changes within human rights, and within particular religions, both of which have increased tensions between the two movements. We now turn to the third ideological development: when these tensions between human rights and religions are exploited for geopolitical ideological benefit. There are two particular examples that illustrate the trend.

The most significant example involves tensions between Islam and the West. No other geopolitical conflict since the end of the Second World War, however important, has involved the relationship between religion and human rights quite so significantly. One example of this general point must suffice. Haynes recounts the attempt of the Organisation of Islamic Cooperation (OIC) to secure a binding UN Resolution condemning 'defamation of religions'.

> The issue was first raised in 1999, and over the next dozen years the OIC led the campaign. Over time, the measure, which was initially widely, albeit rather vaguely, supported by many UN members, including non-Muslim-majority countries, became highly controversial, and no agreement was achievable. The issue developed into an increasingly polarized confrontation involving, on one side, the OIC, Muslim states, and some Muslim FBOs [Faith-based Organizations], such as the Muslim World League. Opposing the pro-defamations of religion coalition was an alliance of Western states and non-state actors, including secular NGOs and FBOs.

Both sides used human rights arguments to support their positions.

Even before the events of 9/11, conflicts between Islamic values and, for example, the ECHR had resulted in considerable doubt being cast on the consistency of sharia with (European) fundamental rights. Post 9/11, however, these issues have been considered in an even more unfavourable light, one where militant Islam is seen by some as posing a threat to national security as well as Enlightenment values in many Western states. The intensity of the debate, and the apparent irresolvability of the disputes, have contributed significantly to Islamic practices in several Western states, such as the way some Muslim women dress, coming before national and international adjudicatory bodies.

Conflicts between religion and human rights have also been the focus of even broader geopolitical activism aimed at securing (or resisting, depending on your viewpoint) ideological hegemony. Attempts have been made by some states to reorient the interpretation of human rights principles in such a way as to make them more sympathetic to religious concerns. One extreme version of the expression of this approach is to be found in the speech by the Russian Orthodox Metropolitan Kirill to the Human Rights Council in March 2008. Metropolitan Kirill claimed that a close identity exists between the appeal of human rights and the central tenets of Christianity. Christianity, indeed, was seen as the origin of the values that are now expressed in human rights documents. He claimed that the development and implementation of human rights principles, such as human dignity, are increasingly diverging from their original grounding in religious values, as attempts are made to separate them from their origins, and religion is becoming marginalized and privatized. The influence of 'extreme feministic views and homosexual attitudes', together with the increasingly important role of a small group of experts and NGOs, meant that the approach of those whose role it is to develop and interpret human rights norms increasingly diverges from the opinion of religious believers, and the moral norms accepted by most people. Instead, he argued, the way in which human rights is interpreted should not privilege any particular national approach to the implementation of human rights but should, instead, recognize that different nations have different experiences, and different histories, which also need to be taken into account in the development of national human rights systems.

Russia's role in supporting this turn was not a given, since it had not previously seemed particularly attracted to such a strong sovereigntist position. Indeed, following the collapse of Communism and the adoption of reforms that embraced constitutional rights, there was a strong push for Russia to join the major international human rights regimes, including the Council of Europe and the ECHR. These were seen as indications of Russia's acceptance of universal human rights after the dark days of Stalinist repression. Since that first flush of enthusiasm, however, Russia has seen much dirty linen being displayed before international and regional human rights bodies. This has resulted in a string of findings of human rights violations, particularly by the European Court of Human Rights (ECtHR). Coming at a time when Russia is strongly reasserting its national interests internationally, and reinventing a narrative of national sovereignty, the external scrutiny of human rights bodies and their 'interference' are perceived as threatening and unwelcome.

Although these concerns covered the gamut of human rights issues, decisions by the ECtHR on issues touching on religion were particularly sensitive because of the increased importance of the Orthodox Church in Russia, after the fall of Communism. Not only was the Russian *government* increasingly antagonistic to the trend of human rights interpretation at the regional and international level, the Russian Orthodox Church was an enthusiastic ally in its scepticism, particularly over issues concerning sexual morality, women's rights, and the family. The *Lautsi* case, in which Italy was required to defend the practice of displaying the crucifix in a public school before the ECtHR, was a key galvanizing moment. The Chamber decision holding the display to be contrary to the ECHR was overturned by the Grand Chamber after significant pressure from an ecumenical coalition of Christian Churches, including the Orthodox Church, apparently demonstrating that public engagement and active participation in litigation could, on occasion, turn the secular human rights tide.

Several recent Resolutions of the UN Human Rights Council, proposed by Russia at the initiative of the Russian Orthodox Church, attempt to have the notion of 'traditional values' accepted into international human rights discourse, and indirectly into human rights interpretation by judges and others. They seek to have concepts at the heart of human rights law, in particular 'dignity', 'freedom', and 'responsibility' interpreted through the lens of the idea of 'traditional values', which is left undefined. Traditional values are seen, then, as the foundation for the pursuit of global human rights. The family, community, society, and educational institutions are identified as having an important role in maintaining and passing on such traditional values. States are called on to strengthen their role through adopting adequate positive measures. In particular, dignity is seen, in these Resolutions, as having the potential to rebalance international human rights back towards the local and the indigenous, weakening the pull of a homogenizing, universal, and liberal ideological agenda. In particular, as we have seen from the speech of Metropolitan Kirill, the aim is particularly to reverse human rights developments in the area of gender and LGBT rights. For Russia to be seen to be leading the charge against what is characterized as Western human rights imperialism strengthens its position as a leader in challenging Western ideology more broadly.

MIGRATION AND CHANGING PERCEPTIONS OF RELIGIOUS DIVERSITY: THE BRITISH EXAMPLE

The fourth development contributing to tensions, increased migration flows, is not strictly an ideological development, but it is a significant part of the ideological story. The ideological conflicts discussed up to this point become more salient due to migration. It is difficult to capture this development at a high level of generality because different countries have very different experiences. A brief case study, I hope, may serve to illustrate the general point I am making. Let's take Britain as an example.

Britain has always been an area of extensive migration, and that migration has often brought different religions into British society, leading sometimes to considerable tensions. In the period before international human rights norms, the relationship between the state and religions, other than the established Church of England, was governed by a considerable degree of political pragmatism and adaptation.

Beginning at least from the early nineteenth century with Catholic Emancipation, a set of political compromises was worked out to accommodate the conflicting interests of the various Christian denominations, and subsequently Judaism, with each other and within an evolving liberal and secular society. Two features of this approach were of particular importance. In the courts, there was a general 'hands off' approach taken to issues that were likely to drag the judges into areas of religious controversy; these issues were thought to be best left to the legislature. In the legislature, the compromises reached were often highly detailed and nuanced; the approach taken to addressing controversies over the role of religion in primary and second education, and the complex arrangements for marriage, were cases in point, as were the detailed rules relating to the way in which ritual animal slaughter was regulated. This approach concentrated heavily on negotiation between those considered to be the religious leaders of the communities concerned, and civic society as represented by the government. This approach proved to be relatively stable, if also relatively lacking in grand principle.

During the 1950s and 1960s, migration occurred which was of a somewhat different character and it resulted in a somewhat different response. Although the British Empire and colonialism were ending, strong ties continued to exist with many former colonies through common membership in the Commonwealth. When economic or political difficulties resulted in migration from these Commonwealth countries, the United Kingdom was frequently seen as a natural refuge, resulting in significant immigration from East Africa (especially Uganda and Kenya) and the Indian subcontinent. These immigrants were often Muslim or Hindu, introducing a relatively new dimension into British society.

Initially, however, it was not the different religious dimension of the new immigrants that was the focus of attention (and tension) but their different ethnic origins and cultural practices. These tensions resulted in significant discrimination in employment, housing, and other aspects of public life and, sometimes, public order problems. As a result, the Labour government of Harold Wilson (in particular under the influence of the then Home Secretary Roy Jenkins) introduced a set of provisions in the mid-1960s to address these tensions, in part by restricting immigration, and in part by adopting a policy of multiculturalism, as it subsequently became known.

A new set of provisions, influenced by statutory developments in the United States, was introduced in this 'multicultural' phase of British politics, beginning around the mid-1960s. While the meaning of 'multiculturalism' is exceedingly difficult to pin down, we can define it as a 'broad set of mutually reinforcing approaches or methodologies concerning the incorporation and participation of immigrants and ethnic minorities and their modes of cultural/religious difference'. Multiculturalism focused, in particular, on developing an approach to the integration into British society of the 'new' ethnic groups increasingly represented in the British population. This relied on a combination of legally enforced anti-discrimination policies in the areas of race and ethnicity, combined with legislative accommodation of what were considered to be ethnocultural practices associated with these major 'new' ethnic groups.

A classic example of the application of these approaches was the judicial and legislative response to the wearing of turbans by Sikh males. A decision by a Church of England school prohibiting a Sikh pupil wearing a turban to school rather than the authorized school uniform was held to amount to unlawful ethnic discrimination by the highest court in the land. The legislative accommodations approach led to an exemption for turban-wearing Sikhs from the otherwise compulsory wearing of helmets when riding a motorcycle. Issues such as these were thought of as primarily racial or ethnic issues, and because in practice (although not in theory) the application of this approach was confined to a relatively discrete set of 'ethnic' practices and groups, they were not considered to have much, if any, relevance to the earlier, pre-multicultural type of accommodations involving Judeo-Christian practices and beliefs. These earlier approaches continued largely unaffected.

Since the beginning of the twenty-first century, however, there have been several developments that have caused both the pre-multicultural and later multicultural accommodations to be rethought, leading to a third phase. There has, in particular, been a significant change in how the earlier ethnocultural practices are now classified; the previous discourse (regarding such practices as 'cultural' or 'ethnic') shifted to focus much more on the *religious* dimension of the practices. This has been encouraged by the increased attention given to Islamic practices, which proved difficult to classify as 'ethnic'. 'British discourse on racialized minorities', wrote Peach in 2005, 'has mutated from "colour" in the 1950s and 1960s, to "race" in the 1960s–1980s, "ethnicity" in the 1990s, and "religion" in the present period.' As Grillo argues, this shift has been one that characterized the self-perception of minority ethnic groups themselves, and coincided with a marked preference among policymakers in government. This was true not only in the context of developments within and reactions to Islamic groups, but also with respect to Hindus and Sikhs.

This change to viewing issues through the lens of religion rather than ethnicity has been accompanied by a growing perception that the earlier approach to how far these beliefs or practices should be accommodated may be in tension with, or at least should be constrained by, core liberal principles. The application of an anti-discrimination approach to issues of religion was merely one of several developments that elevated issues of equality, particularly status equality, to become a central element of liberal modernization. Many of the new social movements that grew up since the 1960s articulated their demands in equality terms. Think of the movements for racial equality, gender equality, disability rights, and LGBT rights. Several of these movements came into conflict with aspects of organized religious practice, in particular those concerning gender and LGBT rights.

As importantly, global events intervened. There has never been a shortage of British critics of multiculturalism, but it is clear that at least since the early years of this century, and certainly since the terrorist attacks of 9/11 in the United States, and July 2005 in London, multiculturalism has faced mounting populist criticism. Some have seen this as heralding the death of multiculturalism and the substitution of a new post-multiculturalism considerably more hostile to certain practices associated with ethnic minorities and immigrants. This unease about the role of religion in public life is not confined to the scrutiny of what were earlier seen as 'ethnic', now 'ethno-religious', practices.

The increased attention to religion as such, has also led to an increase in the scrutiny of *Judeo-Christian* religious practices previously accommodated in the pre-multicultural phase. And this just at a time when a newly resurgent (if limited) Judeo-Christian religious commitment among sections of the population has encouraged individuals outside, as well as inside, the main 'ethnic' groups to assert what they perceive as their religious identity in public. This, too, has led to the manifestation of practices or beliefs in the Judeo-Christian tradition in the public domain coming into conflict with liberal (or simply secular) values. Sometimes, the contested belief or practice is one that is personal to the individual and not necessarily shared in common with an organized church. But sometimes the practice or belief is one that is perceived to be central to an organized religion and is shared in common by significant numbers of those who identify as members of that organized religion.

Criticism of multiculturalism, therefore, has become entwined with criticism of the role of religion in the public domain more generally. Criticism of the attempt by the Archbishop of Canterbury to stimulate debate about the appropriateness of allowing aspects of sharia law to operate in Britain was frequently expressed in terms of the incompatibility of Islam with liberal values of equality, as well as fears that he was encouraging separateness. The shift to favour a wider variety of faith schools, particularly since 1997, has also been a central area of contention, with faith schools being criticized on much the same terms as multiculturalism more generally has been. They are seen as encouraging social division, promoting intolerance, operating as seedbeds of religious fundamentalism, and thus in conflict with current British liberal values.

The fact that principles seen as fundamentally liberal in character have now been incorporated into British law in the Human Rights Act 1998 and (partly as a result of EU law) in equality law has led to these tensions being addressed by the *judiciary*, and has also led to the judicial scrutiny of compromises that were central to earlier phases. This has resulted in several religious or 'ethnic' practices that would be likely to have been accommodated in the multicultural phase now being questioned on the basis of their perceived conflict, for example, with the principle of women's equality. Most prominently, there have been several cases dealing with the wearing of Islamic dress, and their acceptability in a society commitment to the principle of gender equality, not least, of course, in the ECHR.

3

INSTITUTIONS

Mention of the European Court of Human Rights (ECtHR) at the end of the last chapter leads us to the second major set of explanations as to why courts have come to be seen as attractive forums in which to address tensions between religion and secular human rights, namely institutional developments. One development is the greater availability of courts with a human rights jurisdiction. A second factor is the growth of secular NGOs, and parallel changes in organized religions' organizational forms and political organization, both of which have contributed to the increased prevalence of religious litigation domestically and transnationally. A third contributing development is the growth of intra-religious factionalism, involving claims that one group's doctrinal position is the more authentic or authoritative expression of a particular organized religion than that of another group within the same religion. State authorities are then put in the position of having to decide which group to engage with as the true representative of the organized religion, and the courts are called in to adjudicate.

AVAILABILITY OF COURTS

One of the most obvious features of the landscape of religious litigation has been the increasing number of courts that are now open to receiving and adjudicating disputes between human rights and religious beliefs. National courts adjudicating constitutional and fundamental rights have significantly increased in both number and importance since 1945, as more and more countries adopt constitutional courts with the power of judicial review. When we add the increased number of regional courts (such as the ECtHR, the Court of Justice of the European Union, the Inter-American Court of Human Rights, and the African Court of Human and

Peoples' Rights), we can see that the number of available forums has exponentially increased.

It is clearly the case that to have religious litigation, there need to be such courts open for business. But to focus simply on the increased *number* of courts is to miss another development which has been, if anything, more important in stimulating religious litigation: the gradual dominance of NGOs as important interlocutors in the formulation of public policy and the implementation of human rights.

ROLE OF NGOS IN HUMAN RIGHTS

NGOs now play a central role in human rights discourse and enforcement. This particular organizational form is different from and competes with other, earlier forms of organization, whether elite representation in legislatures, mass organizations, or formal corporatist-style representation. As Sabine Lang puts it, the NGOization of civil society 'refers to the process by which social movements professionalize, institutionalize, and bureaucratize in vertically structured, policy-outcome-oriented organizations that focus on generating issue-specific and, to some degree, marketable expert knowledge or services'. Lang identifies the 'pull' to NGOize as created by various incentives, including legal–bureaucratic, economic, and political factors.

In their path-breaking work, Margaret Keck and Kathryn Sikkink defined networks as 'forms of organization characterized by voluntary, reciprocal, and horizontal patterns of communication and exchange'. One form of network they particularly emphasized was what they described as 'transnational advocacy networks', which they identified as including 'those relevant actors working internationally on an issue, who are bound together by shared values, a common discourse, and dense exchanges of information and services'. NGOs, defined by Benjamin Stachursky as 'private, voluntary, nonprofit, nonviolent groups with formal institutional character and aiming at some form of social change', play a particularly important role in these networks.

At the national level in certain jurisdictions, NGOs, with and without a religious background or orientation, have long played an important *political* role in the development of human rights law relating to religion, such as in the United States. There is now extensive scholarly work also demonstrating convincingly that transnational advocacy networks comprising NGOs have played a significant role in lobbying internationally for human rights in general, and influencing the content of particular international human rights covenants, both generally and as regards the protections for freedom of religion.

More recently, in addition to national NGOs operating in their own jurisdiction, and international NGOs operating internationally, we have seen the development of a new breed of transnational NGOs. These are often based in one jurisdiction, and see themselves as primarily interested in issues within that jurisdiction, but are increasingly intervening in jurisdictions *other* than their own. Organizations such as Human Rights Watch or Amnesty fall into this category.

NGOs, perhaps rather peculiarly, have developed a significant degree of legitimacy and authority in several Western countries, although their legitimacy is increasingly questioned elsewhere. The United Nations Economic and Social Council (ECOSOC) provides an important source of international legitimation. ECOSOC consultative status involves a process of accreditation of the NGO, a process that Rana Lehr-Lehnardt has described as potentially 'lengthy, but ... not complicated'. To be accredited, an NGO 'that is not established by a governmental entity or intergovernmental agreement' must, inter alia, be 'concerned with matters falling within the competence of the Economic and Social Council and its subsidiary bodies'. Its 'aims and purposes' must be 'in conformity with the spirit, purposes and principles' of the UN Charter. It should be 'of recognized standing within the particular field of its competence or of a representative character'. It should 'have a democratically adopted constitution' and 'a representative structure', and 'possess appropriate mechanisms of accountability to its members'. These requirements, according to Lehr-Lehnardt, 'include some elements designed to ensure a certain level of democracy and representation, but they are only weakly, if ever, applied'.

CHANGES IN RELIGIONS' ORGANIZATIONAL FORMS AND POLITICAL ORGANIZATION

The relative success of some NGOs as an organizational form has led to a significant degree of emulation, sometimes in unexpected quarters. Institutionally focused studies of religion have begun to reverse 'a long-standing trend in the social and political science literature to overlook the role of religious actors in the public sphere', and have begun to examine the role that *religious* NGOs play. Julia Berger has defined these as 'formal organizations whose identity and mission are self-consciously derived from the teachings of one or more religious or spiritual traditions and which operates on a nonprofit, independent, voluntary basis to promote and realize collectively articulated ideas about the public good at the national or international level'. New terms have been devised to describe NGOs whose mission is derived from the religious beliefs of their leaders, funders, or staff, and various of them are in current use, such as 'faith-based', 'religious', or 'spiritual' NGOs.

Jeffrey Haynes has studied the international and transnational activities of UN-focused faith-based organizations and identified the recent significant increase in the number of such organizations, 'now amounting to over 300 entities, around 10 per cent of the more than 3,000 non-state entities with institutionalized access to the UN via the Economic and Social Council (ECOSOC)'. There are many reasons for this growth. First, the secularization of the West, including the retreat from using 'objective' philosophical, moral, and religious principles as a basis for political and legal reasoning, has created what religiously inclined activists consider to be a large void in public policy that they have attempted to fill by creating institutions and organizations that reflect these principles. A second factor appears to be the relative ease with which the formal status of NGO can be acquired. Not surprisingly, then, the number of religious and other NGOs has mushroomed.

Faith-based organizations seem to matter. Studies have mapped how faith-based organizations play an increasingly important role in regional and international policymaking fora, such as in the United Nations, as well as in norm-creating contexts, such as in the negotiation of new legal and soft-law texts at the international and regional levels. Although there is no systematic study as yet, there is sufficient evidence derived from case studies of particular events to support a preliminary conclusion that these organizations affect policy outcomes on a sufficiently regular basis for them to be taken seriously at both the national and international levels of policy and norm development. There is, then, a marked trend towards the 'NGOization' of organized religions. Julia Berger suggests that the 'need to connect to higher levels of decision-making and share information has led many religious organizations to seek formal recognition as "NGOs" '.

We should not, however, exaggerate the power of such religious organizations. Resolutions in the Human Rights Council must, for example, be introduced by a state with a seat on the Council, and to pass they must be supported by a majority of states on the Council; states remain in the driving seat. As importantly, religious organizations often must secure a broad base of support among secular NGOs and other faith-based organizations if their initiatives are to stand any real chance of surviving. As Haynes points out: 'Trying to exert such influence is especially problematic when FBOs [faith-based organizations] try and act alone, employing solely religious arguments. To acquire and exercise influence at the UN necessitates that FBOs seek partners and allies, including: other FBOs, secular NGOs, and states.' He continues: 'On their own, FBOs struggle at the UN to be taken seriously, with no automatic right to be heard in global policy debates; in this context, seeking allies to pursue goals is crucial. In addition, FBOs must learn to adapt to UN norms and conventions, in order to be heard and accepted.'

INCREASED PREVALENCE OF DOMESTIC RELIGIOUS LITIGATION

There is growing evidence that the legislative and political role of NGOs, both secular and religious, is now being supplemented by an additional role: the initiation and conduct of, or participation in, *litigation* at the domestic level and beyond. NGOs have learned well from secular human rights NGOs the power that courts have in generating interpretations of existing legal norms that support their policy positions and have sought to expand their activities into regional and domestic litigation in order to secure such favourable interpretations. NGOs, in short, play a prominent role in religious litigation on *both* sides of human rights conflicts.

At the national level, the NGOs involved in domestic litigation are a heterogeneous group. Some are local, while others are transnational. Some are 'conservative' in their approach to issues of law and religion, while others are 'liberal' (terms that will require some further explanation subsequently). Some are specialist NGOs, meaning that they concentrate on issues of law and religion, for example, to the exclusion of other human rights issues, while others are generalist, viewing law and religion issues as part (and possibly a relatively minor part) of the menu of issues with which they engage. Some are established on an ad hoc basis, simply focusing on the particular case or issue before the court with no aim to be involved in the longer term, while others have been involved in human rights issues for some considerable time.

Some NGOs are significantly focused on litigation as their primary modus operandi, while others see litigation as only one of a menu of other techniques that may be used to secure their objectives. Although NGOs may also fulfil other less traditional roles in their dealings with courts, the formal role of NGOs in human rights litigation involving religious issues is evident in three ways: by taking cases in their own name; by financially supporting litigation taken by others or providing support in kind; and by intervening as an amicus curiae (or equivalent) in cases in which the NGO is not involved either as a party itself, or in directly supporting one of the parties. This interest in litigation is neither surprising nor unique to the world of religious litigation.

The United States provides one of the best-developed examples of NGOs' involvement in religious litigation. Litigation specifically by religious groups is not a new development in the United States. Much of the Free Exercise and Establishment Clause jurisprudence was prompted by active litigation by two minority religious groups, Seventh Day Adventists and Jehovah's Witnesses. There has also been long-standing activity by groups that want greater separation of church and state, such as Americans United for Separation of Church and State. The present activity by NGOs differs in two respects from what has gone before: in the sheer number of groups now involved, and in the broad swath of social policy issues they now find themselves litigating. The involvement of NGOs in religious litigation appears to be growing, partly because the growing *number* of NGOs requires each to set itself apart from others in a crowded field, and involvement in litigation may be a useful way of doing so. The growing involvement of such NGOs also has much to do with the growing centrality of US courts in deciding hot-button issues in US political life, particularly those that involve contested issues of the relationship between law and morals. The United States has for some time experienced increasingly bitter political standoffs between 'liberal' and 'conservative' political forces, and this has been particularly evident in controversies on issues such as abortion, same-sex marriage, healthcare, gun control, capital punishment, affirmative action, the treatment of immigrants, the issue of torture in the interrogation of suspected terrorists, and the role of religion in public life, to name but a few of the more contentious issues. All of these issues have ended up before the federal judiciary.

Two recent examples of the phenomenon of extensive NGO activity in religious litigation must suffice. In *Lawrence* v. *Texas*, the case in which the US Supreme Court decided that state laws criminalizing sodomy was unconstitutional under federal law, thirty-one amicus briefs were submitted to the Supreme Court, some in favour of upholding the criminalization of sodomy as constitutional (sixteen) and some against (fifteen). In *Hosanna Tabor* v. *EEOC*, the Supreme Court held in a unanimous decision that the Establishment and Free Exercise Clauses barred suits brought on behalf of ministers against their churches, claiming termination in violation of employment discrimination laws. Twenty amicus briefs, many of them from NGOs supporting the application of the ministerial exception, were filed.

There are at least three factors explaining the growing involvement in US courts of religious conservative NGOs. First, conservative religious groups have been increasingly willing to enter the *political* fray, a tendency which is characteristic of a more general trend among conservative groups in the United States and litigation is often seen as a natural extension of political campaigning. Second, other groups with which religious groups share something of an overlapping set of concerns, such as conservative legal networks not involved in religiously related issues, have increasingly turned to the courts in pursuit of their goals, and a degree of emulation can be identified. Third, and most importantly, religious groups consider that they have been forced into a litigious posture because secular NGOs (e.g. the American Civil Liberties Union (ACLU) and American's United for Separation of Church and State) have been effective in using litigation to pursue their agendas.

Of these developments, the growth of a US 'conservative' legal network forms an essential backdrop to the development of a US 'conservative' *religious* legal network. Several recent studies have set out in convincing detail how groups have been established since the 1970s, and particularly during the Reagan and Bush presidencies, to counter the ability of 'liberal' legal groups to change the direction of US law in a more liberal direction, including in such areas as racial equality, personal privacy, women's rights, criminal justice, voting reform, and reproductive rights. Steven Teles has shown how, having failed to translate electoral victory (such as the election of Ronald Reagan) into effective political change, in part because of the perceived liberal bias in the courts, foundations, and groups promoting conservative ideas built a network designed to dislodge legal liberalism from US elite institutions, such as elite law schools and the judiciary. Conservative legal advocacy groups were established to emulate their liberal forebears, using similar tactics.

A note of caution must be sounded, however. The broad-brush distinction drawn above between 'liberal' and 'conservative' is not particularly well chosen, and may well be misleading if the characterization is thought to indicate that interventions are intended to pursue a Republican or Democratic political agenda. It is, unfortunately, almost impossible *not* to use the liberal–conservative distinction, given how pervasive it is in current US political discourse, but many of those who advocate for religious freedom issues do not think they are pursuing a 'conservative' agenda. They view themselves as pro-religious freedom, and pro-human rights *in general*.

A better characterization, perhaps, is to view the controversies as ones within constitutional and human rights law, arising from the clash of human rights, especially the clash between freedom of religion, association, and speech on the one hand (attracting 'conservative' support), and non-discrimination, equality, or personal autonomy norms on the other (attracting 'liberal' support). In the context of this essay, therefore, the terms 'conservative' and 'liberal' have specialized meanings, indicating broadly different orientations on which rights should have priority, and how particular rights should be interpreted.

Although there are few, if any, jurisdictions with so extensive a system of civil society organizations involved in religious litigation as in the United States, a similar trend appears to be emerging in several other countries. Courts and legal procedures outside the United States increasingly mirror the general welcome that NGOs are given in US courts. The pattern of activity will vary depending on several factors such as differing cultural preferences for operating via NGOs, the extent to which litigation is central to political debate, the ease with which NGOs are able to identify relevant cases in which to intervene in a timely manner, and technical court rules determining access to courts by organizations. Indeed, NGOs originating in the US environment seek to have US understandings of how NGOs operate transplanted into their new local environment. Technical rules governing access, in particular the development of amicus curiae interventions, have been developed by US-based NGOs in several of these cases to enable them to be given greater access than those foreign courts would usually accord.

The involvement in religious litigation of NGOs at the domestic level in some other European jurisdictions, such as in the British domestic context, is particularly apparent. In some cases, there are extensive 'interventions' by third parties, a procedure partly popularized by human rights NGOs in the 1990s. This can be seen in *Jivraj* v. *Hashwani*, the case dealing with the legality of specifying the religion of international commercial arbitrators, and in *JFS*, the case challenging a Jewish school's refusal to admit a pupil on the ground that he was not Jewish under the Orthodox Jewish definition. In other cases, equivalent organizations are not just interveners but are the named parties. In the *Christian Institute* case, an application for judicial review of the making of regulations prohibiting discrimination on grounds of sexual orientation, the plaintiffs were seven religiously based organizations.

TRANSNATIONAL NGO LITIGATION

Religiously affiliated groups now use interventions in domestic courts to attempt to embed particular models of religious rights, but NGOs are increasingly also operating on a transnational basis, identifying litigation opportunities to promote their ideological positions wherever they occur, and this jurisdictional opportunism may carry them well outside their own jurisdictions. Again, this development mirrors an equivalent development in liberal NGOs. Religiously affiliated NGOs are attempting to get into the 'intervention game' that more secular NGOs had already made their own. Political science scholarship has long detailed how liberal human rights NGOs engage in extensive national and international activity in support of their ideals. Religiously affiliated NGOs are relative latecomers to this game, attempting to 'catch up' with the practices of secular NGOs in their national jurisdictions, and taking advantage of globalization to tackle the secularizing effects of modernization in other jurisdictions as well.

Three examples illustrate this development. First, the European Centre for Law and Justice (ECLJ), which was established as the European arm of the American Center for Law and Justice, has intervened in litigation before the Slovak Constitutional Court challenging a law permitting abortion up to twelve weeks, at the request of the pregnant woman. Second, the US-based groups Advocates International and the Alliance Defense Fund (ADF) were involved in supporting Pastor Åke Green in resisting criminal conviction in Sweden for a sermon that was alleged to be homophobic. This support included submitting (apparently influential) amicus briefs to the Swedish Supreme Court on his behalf, an initiative that was joined by several other foreign interveners, including the Becket Fund, the Family Research Council, Focus on the Family, the (Canadian) Christian Legal Fellowship, and the (British) Jubilee Campaign. Third, in Romania, when the Constitutional Court was petitioned to validate a referendum seeking to constitutionalize a ban on same-sex marriage, ADF filed a brief supporting a local NGO (the Alliance of Romania's Families, modelled on equivalent US NGOs). The brief argued that the proposed amendment was constitutional, drawing in part on European Union law. This was countered by a brief from another local NGO, ACCEPT, also with overseas backing, citing international standards as prohibiting the proposed amendment.

The well-known 'culture wars' clash in the United States between civil society actors, borrowing from the German expression for the dispute between Bismarck and the Catholic Church in the nineteenth century, has now gone transnational. US conservative groups (including faith-based NGOs) have begun to emulate strategies earlier developed by liberal groups, and NGOs now face off against each other politically across the globe. Many of the same protagonists, particularly NGOs that find themselves against each other in US courts, now find new litigation opportunities abroad in which to fight their battles *against each other*. As Bob has observed: 'most global issues involve not just a single "progressive" movement promoting a cause, but also rivals fighting it'. 'Global civil society', he continues, 'is not a harmonious field of like-minded NGOs. It is a contentious arena riven by fundamental differences crisscrossing national and international boundaries.'

Interventions by NGOs in transnational religious litigation appear to be on the increase due to a combination of political and legal reasons. One reason is that human rights NGOs have frequently adopted an understanding of constitutional and human rights that is universalist and cosmopolitan and this has the effect of encouraging a view that violations of rights in one country are as much the NGO's business as violations in any other country. A second reason is an acceptance of the fact that globalization means that what happens in another country may well directly or indirectly affect developments in the NGO's own country—a favourable decision in one jurisdiction may 'cascade', influencing developments in other jurisdictions, and then globally. A third element in the story is that one way of appealing to their domestic audience is for domestic NGOs to intervene in litigation in foreign courts against policies and practices that are particularly unpopular in the NGOs' home jurisdiction.

Regional human rights courts, in particular the ECtHR, have proved particularly important forums for these purposes, and a similar pattern of NGO participation in religious litigation to that seen in domestic litigation has been apparent in these courts for some time, and on similar issues. In the *Lautsi* litigation before the ECtHR, for example, in which the Court considered whether Italian public schools could keep the crucifix despite objections by a parent, leave to intervene was given to several NGOs. As well as expressing their views on issues of religious freedom, interveners in cases before the ECtHR have been particularly prominent in cases concerning abortion, and sexual orientation. In *A, B and C* v. *Ireland*, considering Ireland's ban on abortion, numerous third-party submissions were received. In *X* v. *Austria*, a case claiming the right of same-sex couples to adopt, joint third-party comments were received on behalf of six NGOs. Third-party comments were also received from (among others) the ECLJ (which also intervened in *Lautsi*), and ADF, now renamed Alliance Defending Freedom, which had each been given leave to intervene in the written procedure.

It is a noticeable feature of *religious* transnational litigation that it is, in the main, US *conservative* NGOs which are at the forefront of this development, a phenomenon that warrants a brief explanation. After *Lawrence*, the ECtHR has been a particular target for interventions. The largest group of NGOs active before the court is based in the United Kingdom, but the second largest group of NGOs comes from the United States, including several that are law school clinics, and a significant proportion of that group of US NGOs is made up of religious conservative groups. In the ECtHR, the ECLJ and the ADF are particularly evident, but the Becket Fund, American United for Life, the International Center for Law and Religion Studies of Brigham Young University, and the Family Research Council have all intervened at one time or another.

Their involvement abroad is linked to the split between conservative and liberal justices on the US Supreme Court concerning the utility, persuasiveness, and appropriateness of relying on foreign precedents. In *Lawrence*, over strident dissents, the majority opinion of the US Supreme Court partially relied on ECtHR jurisprudence to find unconstitutional the criminalization of sodomy under state law. Since *Lawrence*, US-based conservative NGOs see European decisions as potentially undermining their position in US courts. Some US NGOs thus litigate in Europe partly in the hope of staving off decisions that may come back to haunt them when similar issues are litigated in the US. Bob quotes the chief counsel of ADF, Benjamin Bull: 'We're forced to do it, because if we don't, we're going to lose according to rules of a game we never created.' As Bob put it, their objectives are pre-emptively to forge 'overseas law into something less dangerous, more ambiguous, or downright helpful'.

Interventions seem partly to be based on the idea that, following *Lawrence*, one way of instantiating a particular model of accommodation with resurgent religion *in the United States* is therefore to ensure 'favourable' decisions *by the ECtHR*. It is noteworthy that the ECLJ was established by the American Center for Law and Justice precisely to establish such precedents in the ECtHR. It is not alone. When ADF was granted permission to intervene in the *Eweida* case in the ECtHR, one of the cases joined with *Ladele*, its President and General Counsel described it to supporters as a 'remarkable opportunity ... to stand in defense of religious freedom ... in cases that—if they are decided the wrong way—could have a negative impact on your religious liberty here in the United States'.

Interventions by transnational NGOs have, so far, been relatively uncontroversial in the European context. Where such interventions occur *outside* Europe, however, this has proved more controversial, because it has raised accusations of neo-colonialism that feature much less prominently in the European context. A common pattern of NGO involvement appears to be evolving. Initially, local progressive groups become involved in a particular jurisdiction to reform an aspect of domestic policy or practice, often using the local courts as part of their reform strategy. These efforts are frequently supported by arguments drawing on international law and precedents from other jurisdictions, as well as material and other support from progressive human rights groups outside the jurisdiction. This, in turn, results in those opposing these changes arguing that those advocating change are not only wrong in principle, but that such changes only come about as a result of objectionable outside interference.

The current controversy surrounding the criminalization of sodomy is a prime example. Although not entirely restricted to states with a history of British colonial rule, these states have frequently resorted to criminalization . At least since the decision of the ECtHR in *Dudgeon*, attempting to have such crimes struck down has become an important aspect of the work of groups campaigning in favour of gay rights, often using international law to argue that such legislation is illegitimate. A good example of this is the successful campaign to ensure that the Inter-American Court of Human Rights would decide that criminalization was contrary to the Inter-American Convention on Human Rights. This case attracted interventions from influential lawyers drawing on European human rights law, which the Inter-American Court largely adopted. In India, a similar strategy also led initially to a successful outcome for gay rights campaigners, with the Delhi High Court holding that criminalizing sodomy was contrary to the Indian Constitution, only to see that judgment itself overturned by the Indian Supreme Court.

These actions have, however, led to a counter-reaction, based partly on opposition to change on the basis of principle, but also objecting to what local conservative groups have characterized as a transnational attempt to undermine domestic decisions on issues of morality that are more appropriately left to national decision-making processes. We thus see in several countries attempts to restrict the activities of NGOs, particular foreign-based NGOs, operating in this field. Another effect, however, is that, partly in reaction to the intervention by liberal transnational NGOs, conservative religious groups, many from the United States, not infrequently support local conservative forces.

Having lost the constitutional battle at home to preserve the criminalization of sodomy in *Lawrence*, these US conservative religious groups have turned their attention to other places where equivalent issues are under consideration. This has resulted in interventions at the legislative and policy levels in several developing countries, most controversially in Uganda, where US-based conservatives have been criticized as partly responsible for the backlash against the NGOs that led to the passage of the legislation restricting foreign NGOs. There is often, therefore, significant foreign support for local actors on *both* sides of religiously engaged litigation. We thus increasingly see a standoff occurring, between the local progressive actors and local conservative groups, but also between transnational progressive and transnational conservative groups.

Conservative and liberal transnational NGOs faced each other in the Caribbean, for example, particularly in the case of *Orozco* v. *Attorney General of Belize*, in which the Human Dignity Trust, the International Commission of Jurists, and the Commonwealth Lawyers Association supported a local gay rights activist, Caleb Orozco, the head of United Belize Advocacy Movement, in challenging the constitutionality of the Belize criminal code which criminalizes consensual sexual conduct between adults of the same sex. The case had potential importance beyond Belize, as similar laws were under scrutiny across the Commonwealth Caribbean. They were opposed by a coalition named Church Interested Parties, which included the local Catholic Church in Belize, the Belize Church of England Corporate Body, and the local Evangelical Association of Churches. In addition, there was a local umbrella group, Belize Action, which also supported the existing law.

The issue of outside interventions (on both sides) has been mired in controversy, with criticisms of the Human Dignity Trust for appearing to take over the Orozco's case. On the other side, the Southern Poverty Law Center reported that Belize Action was partly funded by ADF, a US-based religious NGO, a report that a US pastor associated with Belize Action denied, while accepting that ADF had provided advice, legal assistance, and strategic advice.

INTRA-RELIGIOUS (LEGAL) FACTIONALISM

The final institutional development that I want to stress has to do with the fracturing of churches. The issue of factionalism within organized religions, and the extent to which such disputes should be aired in public, is as old as many organized religions themselves, and it remains a fruitful source of religious litigation. Faith-based organizations that associate themselves with a particular religion (sometimes even to the extent of including the name of the religion in their title) end up on opposing sides, whether on policy issues, treaty negotiations, or litigation, with both sides claiming to speak authentically for the religion. Increasingly, too, the disputing factions are labelled externally (and sometimes internally) in secular political terms. Berger, for example, suggests that 'One of the characteristics of present-day denominations is the growing gap separating "liberal" and "conservative" believers.' Haynes has noted how, 'like other sorts of actors at the UN, [FBOs] can be *either* "conservative" or "liberal", and their stance on the issues ... is linked to an ideological view of the world rather than the result of religious characteristics *per se*'. Barnett and Stein have even suggested that NGOs nominally identifying with the same religious tradition may have more ideological variation between themselves than there is between religious and secular NGOs.

The most studied recent example of the phenomenon is that of the Catholic Church's standoff with Catholics for Choice, but the debate over this marginal organization masks the bigger issue. We have already seen that there are significant debates within Catholicism over human rights. Given the differences between 'revisionist' and 'anti-revisionist' approaches, it is not surprising that Catholic understandings of the role of women and of the behaviour of gay men and women, as reflected in the writing of Catholic theologians, reflect a considerably greater plurality of viewpoints than those outside the Church sometimes appear to recognize. In the case of Islamic law, too, various different and conflicting messages are sent, depending on which texts are cited, with texts of the Qur'an and Sunna of the Medina period contrasting with the texts of the Qur'an of the Mecca period. This opens up the opportunity for internal dialogue within both the Catholic and Islamic traditions.

'Liberal' and 'conservative' Muslim groups, for example, were found on both sides of the move to secure UN agreement on a resolution condemning 'defamation of religions' discussed earlier, which was seen at the time as a critical test of Islamic influence. As we have seen, the resolution was supported by a group of Muslim states, the OIC, and several Muslim faith-based NGOs. However, in a high-profile intervention, 186 NGOs signed a petition in March 2009 opposing the resolution. This group included several 'liberal' Muslim NGOs including the Muslim Council of Canada, the Ahmadiyya Muslim Community, Muslims against Sharia, the

Council of ex-Muslims of Britain, the Coalition for Defence of Human Rights in the Muslim World, the American Islamic Congress, and the American Islamic Forum for Democracy. There are several concrete examples that illustrate the phenomenon in action in the domestic context also. In Canada, there was a high-profile dispute over whether a provincial government should establish sharia tribunals to which Muslims could voluntarily submit civil disputes, with the finding of the tribunal being given legal weight. The proposal was supported by the Canadian Islamic Congress (CIC) but opposed by the Muslim Canadian Congress (MCC) and the Canadian Council of Muslim Women, leading to a very public dispute between the MCC and the CIC, with the latter accusing those Muslims who criticized sharia of 'publicly deriding their religion, badmouthing the Prophet, ridiculing the Qur'an and mounting uninformed crusades to smear their Islamic Law, the Shariah'.

For the purposes of this chapter, however, the important point is that this intra-religious factionalism has also contributed to religious issues being brought to courts; not infrequently, one or other side in the internal dispute has resorted to litigation. Such disputes often involve claims by the disputing parties that their position is the more authentic or authoritative expression of the religion to which both claim adherence. As a result, a central area of controversy in the relationship between state law and organized religion on occasion is how state authorities are to decide with whom to engage when there is a dispute as to who represents the organized religion. The state must choose, but how are state authorities to decide what the beliefs of an organized religion are, where this is contested within the religion itself? These disputes have arisen when, for example, there is a schism in a church and the court is asked to decide between the two groups, such as was the case in several nineteenth-century disputes in Scotland when the Church of Scotland split. It may arise when two or more parts of the organized religion compete over questions of who can be a 'member' of the religion, such as the long-running dispute between Orthodox and Reform Judaism over who can be a Jew.

State authorities, and particularly the courts, are increasingly faced with a dilemma in these situations: on the one hand, there is a strong incentive for these authorities to remain 'neutral', to avoid getting involved in what are seen as internal disputes within the religion and not appropriately subject to secular authority; on the other, liberal societies have increasingly sought to inculcate particular human rights norms in their communities, and these norms (such as women's equality, or avoiding discrimination on the basis of sexual orientation) frequently run up against the practices and beliefs of organized religions, whether Christian, Muslim, or Jewish. Both positions are supported by human rights arguments. How is the court to decide between them?

PART II
PROBLEMS

4
THE TELEOLOGICAL PROBLEM

In Part I of the essay, I suggested that there have been several significant ideological and institutional developments that have contributed to domestic and regional courts becoming forums for religious litigation. Those chapters focused, in other words, on why and how religious litigation gets to court. In Part II, I suggest a more complex argument, one more centred on what happens once these cases reach court. Part II comprises three chapters reflecting three problems, the teleological, epistemological, and ontological problems. I'll begin in this chapter with the teleological, then consider the epistemological, and conclude with the ontological. (Some might consider a different ordering of the three problems to be preferable, and they may well be correct in strict logic, but this ordering better serves my heuristic purposes; no theoretical significance should be inferred from the ordering chosen.)

THE TELEOLOGICAL PROBLEM IDENTIFIED

We saw in Chapter 2 that there is a multiplicity of differing ways in which religion is 'addressed' as such, but in essence this diversity of approach resolves into three main approaches: an anti-discrimination/equality approach in which religious discrimination is prohibited, a freedom of religion approach in which the practice of religion is protected, and a third approach that ensures protection from religious coercion. For convenience, I'll refer to the first as the religious discrimination provisions, and the second two as the freedom of religion provisions. These elements are set within the context of human rights systems. They are elements of that system, but also constrained by other parts of the system.

In this section, we turn to the first of the three problems I identified, what I have called 'the teleological problem', that is the

Litigating Religions: An Essay on Human Rights, Courts, and Beliefs. Christopher McCrudden. Published 2018 by Oxford University Press.

problem courts face of deciding what the primary human rights protections relating specifically to religion are for, what their aim or *telos* is. Neither with regard to the freedom of religion provisions, nor with regard to the religious discrimination provisions, is there any real consensus as to what they are aiming to achieve. Are they protecting the vulnerable? Are they to prevent civil strife? Are they another way of protecting minorities? Is there something in the nature of religion that means that these provisions are *sui generis*? The courts have struggled mightily with these issues, and contrasting approaches are to be found within the courts of the same jurisdictions, between the courts of different jurisdictions, and between courts and organized religions themselves.

FREEDOM OF RELIGION

Why are religions worth protecting, and what should the relationship be between the state and religion? Traditionally, this issue has most often been considered in the context of human and constitutional rights protection of 'freedom of religion', which is usually a complex set of permissions and limits on how individuals and groups may 'manifest' their religious beliefs in public. In US constitutional terminology, this tension between permission and restriction is often played out in the First Amendment jurisprudence in the tangled relationship between the 'establishment' and the 'free exercise' clauses, but we shall focus initially on the approaches adopted in the interpretation of freedom of religion in the European Convention on Human Rights (ECHR).

The ECHR contains several different kinds of rights, or at least rights with different weights. So, we can distinguish those rights, such as the right to be free from torture, the right not to be held in slavery, and the right to life, as rights that have very considerable weight. In the case of torture and slavery, we even say that the right is 'absolute' in the sense that the right has such weight that no other consideration is sufficiently important for it to trump that right. Other rights, in particular such rights as the right to a private life, the right to freedom of speech, and the right to freedom of assembly, are structured so that other considerations can be taken into account in determining whether that right has been breached. In that sense, these rights are qualified rather than absolute. 'Qualified' rights are thus highly contextualized, requiring judgements to be made about how the right is to be exercised in particular situations, and the limits on that right.

The right to freedom of religion in the ECHR is partly of the first type, and partly of the second type. The right to 'freedom of thought, conscience and religion' has two dimensions. First, there is the 'freedom to change his religion or belief'; this is not subject to any limitation (we might say it is an 'absolute' right). Second, there is the 'freedom, either alone or in community with others and in public or private, to manifest his religion or belief in worship, teaching, practice and observance'; this is a 'qualified' right, subject to limitations set out in the second part of Article 9 itself. The way in which this limitation provision is drafted (any limitations on the right must be 'necessary in a democratic society') leads the European Court of Human Rights (ECtHR) to test for 'proportionality': that is, the Court considers whether the purpose of the limitation of the right is legitimate, whether the limitation is necessary for attaining that purpose, and whether the measure strikes a proper balance between that purpose and the right that is being restricted.

The inclusion of a right to freedom of religion in both aspects requires explanation and justification, but it is the second aspect on which particular attention has been lavished, because it is the 'manifestation' of religious practice in public that is more likely to meet with opposition, at least in modern circumstances. There is now a sophisticated literature in both law and philosophy discussing why it is, or is not, appropriate to include special protections for freedom of religion as such. What is it about religion that should lead to it being given a specially tailored right? What is the value that a freedom of religion provision protects that can't be equally well catered for by other provisions, such as freedom of speech, privacy, rights to marry, property rights, the right to education, and so forth? Think of it this way: assume, for the moment, that a Bill of Rights guaranteed freedom of association, freedom of speech, and freedom from discrimination (including on grounds of religion), would anything be lost if there were not a provision guaranteeing freedom of religion in the form that we have in the ECHR? For some, of course, there is no good justification for such special protection: religion should stand or fall according to the same standards as other systems of belief and action.

Avoiding civil strife

For those who consider that there is a place for a freedom of *religion* provision, however, one of several different responses tends to be adopted. Freedom of religion is sometimes regarded as special because in the past religious disputes have proved so fractious and divisive that, for the sake of peace, it is inadvisable for the state to intervene in religious controversies unless there is a very strong reason to do so. This concern dates at least from the need to resolve the religious wars that scarred much of the seventeenth and eighteenth centuries in Europe. Guaranteeing freedom of religion was seen as a means of guaranteeing civil peace. For British courts, guaranteeing freedom of religion for this reason remains of current significance. Lord Nicholls, for example, stressed how respecting another's religious beliefs, 'enables [us] to live in harmony. This is one of the hallmarks of a civilized society. Unhappily, all too often this hallmark has been noticeable by its absence. Mutual tolerance has had a chequered history even in recent times. The history of most countries, if not all, has been marred by the evil consequences of religious and other intolerance.'

The potential for civil strife if religious passions are not moderated by mutual tolerance therefore provides an important background consideration against which to interpret the role of freedom of religion. Where courts have a feeling that accepting claims to freedom of religion is likely to increase rather than decrease religious tensions, they tend to react negatively. It is noteworthy, for example, that in upholding the compromise that a school had worked out over which types of Islamic dress to permit, Lord Bingham stressed the 'period of harmony ... to which the uniform policy was thought to contribute', how the compromise was 'acceptable to mainstream Muslim opinion', how the changes proposed by the claimant 'would or might have significant adverse repercussions', and how the Court would be 'irresponsible' to override the school 'on a matter as sensitive as this'. The 'confrontational' and the 'threatening' nature of the way in which the issue was raised by the claimants, and the sense that an 'extremist version of the Muslim religion' might be being promoted, will not have helped the applicant either. In the same case, Lady Hale was even more explicit: 'The school's task is . . . to promote the ability of people of diverse races, religions and cultures to live together *in harmony*.'

Protecting the private sphere

There is a second, alternative argument adopted by those who consider that there is a place for a freedom of *religion* provision: that there is some particular added value that religious freedom protects that the other rights do not, such as the importance of individual conscience, or the value of being reminded of the importance of the spiritual. The parallels between privacy and freedom of religion in this regard are in some ways quite striking. Freedom of religion emphasizes membership in a religion as something that involves *private* beliefs and activity. Indeed, there is much in common more generally between the idea of a zone of privacy and the protection of freedom of religion. The protection of the first aspect of freedom of religion distinguished earlier, the *forum internum* as it is called, has much in common with a privacy idea. Under freedom of religion more generally, the approach taken is one that emphasizes the singular importance of the individual's choice to act on a particular belief. It is similar to deciding whether or not to engage in sexual activity, and of what type, both choices which are regarded as *private* choices. The idea of toleration is also central to both. As with privacy in the sexual orientation context, under freedom of religion judges are not called on to approve the religion or belief that claims protection, simply to be prepared to tolerate it. Freedom of religion, in this justification, protects the free choices of autonomous individuals within a zone of beliefs. One can say that this is the primary understanding of the freedom of religion protected by Article 9 ECHR. Indeed, the Court has said as such: 'religious freedom is *primarily* a matter of individual conscience'.

These aspects of freedom of religion are often seen as involving different elements of what US jurisprudence would call the First Amendment 'free exercise' of religion. We have, however, already identified another aspect of freedom of religion, what we have termed 'freedom *from* religion', or at least freedom from religion imposed as an exercise of state authority. The limited version of this aspect of religious freedom adopted in the ECHR amounts to a requirement that the state should not coerce individuals to adopt a religion, and should not favour one religion over another. The ECtHR has held that national governments cannot unreasonably discriminate between religions with regard to the requirements that the church must fulfil. So, Article 9 safeguards the right of one religion to be free to operate on conditions equal to other churches, especially where the action of the state causes an unjustified restriction on the exercise of religious freedom in its collective dimension.

The relationship between the individual and the collective dimensions is problematic. Understanding the value of freedom of religion as primarily the protection of a zone of privacy is in tension with what we can call the 'collective dimension' of organized religion. The ECtHR has recognized that 'religious communities traditionally and universally exist in the form of organised structures. They abide by rules which are often seen by followers as being of a divine origin.' Indeed, the ECtHR regularly emphasizes that states should not underestimate the importance of the community dimension of the right. While we have seen that the Court said that 'religious freedom is primarily a matter of individual conscience' it went on to say, in the same case, and immediately following this, that Article 9 'also implies, inter alia, freedom to manifest one's religion, alone and in private, or in community with others, in public and within the circle of those whose faith one shares'.

How do the courts address the relationship between the protection of an individual private right, and claims based on the protection of this collective dimension? The answer, unfortunately, is 'in some confusion', and in a multiplicity of voices. One approach is to seek to individualize the collective dimension. Freedom of religion in its collective dimension is seen as important partly because it furthers the autonomy of the individual. So, the Court has said that: 'the autonomous existence of religious *communities* . . . directly concerns . . . the effective enjoyment of the right to freedom of religion by all its active *members*. Were the organisational life of the community not protected by Article 9 of the Convention, all other aspects of the *individual's* freedom of religion would become vulnerable.'

Pluralism

In other cases, however, the Court considers that freedom of religion in both its individual and collective aspects is important for a third main reason, that such freedom is in the interests of the society as a whole, not just in the interests of the individual believer or collectively organized religion. In particular, the Court has viewed the collective aspect of freedom of religion as going beyond safeguarding the particular religious community in question, considering that 'it is also a precious asset for atheists, agnostics, sceptics and the unconcerned. The pluralism indissociable from a democratic society, which has been dearly won over the centuries, depends on it.' 'Indeed', the Court says, 'the autonomous existence of religious communities is indispensable for pluralism in a democratic society and is thus an issue at the very heart of the protection which Article 9 affords'. For the ECtHR, it is important to protect 'the dynamics of cultural traditions, ethnic and cultural identities, religious beliefs, artistic, literary and socio-economic ideas and concepts'. To repeat, this does not mean that the state (or the Court) is called on to approve the religious beliefs; it is the existence of the variety of beliefs that is important, presumably irrespective of whether they are 'correct' or not.

This approach to its collective dimension brings Article 9 closer to freedom of association and freedom of expression than it does to privacy because of the public nature of the association and the perceived value of the diversity of expression that is protected. As the Court has said: 'Where the organization of the religious community is at issue, Article 9 must be interpreted in the light of Article 11 of the Convention which safeguards associative life against unjustified State interference. Seen in this perspective, the believer's right to freedom of religion encompasses the expectation that the community will be allowed to function peacefully free from arbitrary State intervention.' The Court refers to this freedom from arbitrary intervention in the collective dimension of the freedom as protecting the 'autonomy' of the religious institution.

Perhaps the most powerful instances in which the ECtHR has found a violation of the collective dimension of Article 9 relate to the Court's refusal to permit states to interfere in the choice of leaders of particular churches. In a series of cases, the ECtHR has held that the state must ensure that religious organizations retain autonomy in relation to the selection of their own leaders. The Court has held, for example, that Article 9 was violated because of Bulgaria's 'interference with the internal organization of the Muslim community'. Several of these 'leadership' cases concern disputes between different parts of the religious community, where the state has sided with one section of the community by appointing the religious leader directly. When differences within or between religious groups lead to tensions, the Court has affirmed that the 'role of the authorities in such circumstances is not to remove the cause of the tension by eliminating pluralism', meaning that the state should not attempt to solve the problem by imposing one view (or leader) on the whole religious community. In a particularly important example of this approach, the Court said: 'State measures favouring a particular leader or specific organs of a divided religious community or seeking to compel the community or part of it to place itself, against its will, under a single leadership, would also constitute an infringement of the freedom of religion.'

In an intra-religious community dispute, when it is open to one group to establish alternative ways of achieving their aim, then the solution most appropriate to ensuring pluralism is for that group to pursue the alternative, rather than to insist that the other group change its practices.

Relationship between these justifications

We can see, therefore, that there are three main approaches that characterize the ECHR's interpretation of Article 9: an approach based on maintaining civil peace; an approach based on securing protection of private choices; and an approach based on ensuring the pluralism of the public space. The Court draws on each of these in its jurisprudence but has never, to my knowledge, made clear which, if any, has priority over the others, and the precise relationship between them remains largely unresolved.

As if that were not confusing enough, the approaches adopted in the European human rights context are now significantly different from those adopted in the US constitutional context. Two competing approaches may be identified, one involving separation of religion and state (which traces its lineage back to Thomas Jefferson's metaphor of a wall of separation between church and state), and the other permitting a greater degree of accommodation of religion by the state.

In the first approach, the issue is often how high or impregnable the wall should be, rather than whether there should be a wall at all. The idea behind separation is simple enough. Shifting metaphors, if we appeal to the jurisdictional metaphor of spheres of autonomy or sovereignty, the separationist approach imagines two spheres, one representing the state and the other representing religion, although this simple picture is quickly rendered more complex when the reality of many religious orbs, rather than one, is recognized.

In the second approach, the motivating idea is that the goal of separation is itself misguided; that religion and the state do not represent opposing parties who must maintain a wall to keep boundaries clear. It rejects the dictum that 'good walls make good neighbours'. Rather, the accommodationist approach posits that there is and should be an element of coexistence and co-influence, even co-maintenance, between religion (or some religions) and the state. This approach may warm into an attitude of cooperation, although in an era of increasing religious diversity, which religions to include within this welcoming web of mutual assistance is likely to become controversial. And the risk of cooperation between church and state, leading to one being co-opted by the other, is a recurring problem.

Neither of these approaches is adopted wholesale in either the United States or the ECHR, but it is probably true to say that the separationist approach is closer to current US First Amendment doctrine, while the accommodationist approach is closer to the ECtHR's position. But we should not regard either of these models as set in stone in the respective jurisdiction. The position in each jurisdiction discussed continues to evolve, and it is conceivable that the interpretation in each could move closer to the other. For example, will the European Court be willing to police a state that *prohibits* religious symbols in the public space? Will the Court be willing to consider such restrictions to be disproportionate on the grounds that they manifest coercion against particular religions? More particularly, if these bans are not considered to be coercive but simply to have adopted a secularist point of view, how will the Court go about the task of testing whether the overall context of the ban manifests neutrality or hostility? What, in other words, is the social meaning of the restrictions, and to whom?

Uncertainty within each jurisdiction breeds the type of litigation that we discussed briefly in Chapter 1; the availability of competing models between jurisdictions breeds the type of transnational litigation we considered in Chapter 3.

PROTECTION FROM RELIGIOUS DISCRIMINATION

The assumption is often made that issues of religious conscience arise only in the context of freedom of religion/free exercise claims: an individual with a conscientious belief argues that the guarantee that we are free to practise our religion means that laws that require us to contravene our conscience should be limited, or overridden, or set aside: the conscientious believer should be granted an exemption. This framing of the issue means that the conflict is a relatively straightforward one between freedom of religion and, for example, freedom from discrimination on the grounds of sexual orientation. There have, indeed, been several high-profile cases that have been formulated in just this way, and the conflicts between equality and freedom of religion that are generated are complex and multifaceted. In some jurisdictions, this may, indeed, be the principal way in which the issues will be framed.

But, at least in the European context, to conceive the problem of religious conscience *only* in this way is misleading, and evades an even more difficult issue. Recently, much more attention has been given to the relationship between conscience and discrimination in a way that generates tensions *within* the concepts of equality and discrimination themselves. This is because, increasingly, the claim to protection by the conscientious believer is formulated in anti-discrimination terms rather than (or sometimes in addition to) freedom of religion terms: the claim is that by requiring me to conform to an anti-discrimination requirement that prohibits racial or gender or sexual orientation, you discriminate against me on religious grounds. In this chapter, I shall be focusing, therefore, on conflicts within equality that are generated by claims to the protection of religious conscience formulated as religious discrimination claims.

The fact that arguments concerning the place of religion in the public or private spheres are now frequently reframed in practice as issues of 'discrimination' and 'equality' appears to result from at least two significant developments. The first is that legal practitioners now more frequently identify anti-discrimination arguments as providing ways of avoiding the uncertainties engendered by the jurisprudence on freedom of religion. The second is that the growth of equality and discrimination arguments generally, and in particular the greater focus on the protection of various identities, has brought to the fore the 'identity' dimensions of religion. But is the 'telos' of an anti-discrimination approach any clearer or more defined than that of 'freedom of religion'?

Several similarities between freedom of religion and freedom from discrimination on the basis of religion are initially quite striking. There is, in particular, a degree of overlap between the interpretation of freedom of religion and the religious discrimination provisions in so far as freedom of religion itself encompasses an equality dimension. We have seen, for example, that freedom of religion has been interpreted as encompassing a degree of equality between religions. Indeed, one of the ways in which a breach of freedom of religion is proven is by pointing to more favourable treatment being accorded to another religion when, other things being equal, they should have been treated similarly. This intuition is captured in the ECHR through Article 14, the original intention of which was to provide that substantive rights should not be delivered in a discriminatory way.

Beyond these similarities, however, textual differences emerge. In Article 9, freedom of religion (along with thought, conscience, and belief) is singled out for special treatment, in the sense that freedom of religion has a particular provision that is devoted primarily to enunciating this freedom, whereas the provision prohibiting religious discrimination is located among several other grounds for non-discrimination, including race, gender, etc. A second difference is more institutional—unlike the treatment of 'freedom of religion', freedom from religious discrimination has, in the past, often been the subject of detailed legal treatment in ordinary statute law as well as being sometimes addressed through constitutional or human rights provisions.

In light of this, there are two major problems in identifying the *telos* of the anti-discrimination approach when applied to religion. The first is the relationship between 'freedom of religion' and 'freedom from religious discrimination'. Is there anything *fundamentally* distinctive between these rights? Do the differences in drafting and institutional elaboration discussed above denote a significant substantive difference? Or do the two rights seek to do essentially the same thing? In short, does it matter whether an issue is presented as one of freedom of religion, or one of religious discrimination?

The second problem arises from concerns about the internal coherence of the protectorate included in anti-discrimination law. Anti-discrimination law frequently prohibits discrimination against an expanding list of protected categories. We might seek to explain the inclusion of religion as a protected category simply as the result of interest-group lobbying, political influence, and historical contingency, but even if that approach accounts for the development in a way that convinces historians and political scientists, it has not proved sufficient for lawyers and judges, who tend to assume that, if there is a list, then there is some principled connection between the grounds protected that goes beyond historical contingency and politics.

Relationship between 'freedom of religion' and 'freedom from discrimination'

I'll consider, first, the relationship between 'freedom of religion' and 'freedom from discrimination'.

The differences between the two rights do appear to have been recognized, at least to a limited extent, in legislative drafting. In both European Union and UK anti-discrimination law, there are several exceptions to the religious anti-discrimination provisions aiming to ensure that freedom of religion is not breached, thus indicating that the two rights are thought to incorporate different principles. But the differences between these provisions are more fundamental than simply differences in drafting style, material scope, legal source, and limitations, however important these are in practice.

First, the discrimination provisions are essentially comparative. The approach adopted to the interpretation of the religious discrimination provision emphasizes the nature of discrimination as involving the less favourable treatment of one person *in comparison* with another person, based on the differences in their religion. We saw that approach being adopted by the Court in *Ladele*. Freedom of religion protections, on the other hand, are not seen as *essentially* comparative. There can be a breach of a provision guaranteeing freedom of religion, irrespective of the same treatment being accorded (or not accorded) to adherents of all other religions, or, indeed, everyone else. Freedom of religion, at least in theory, protects the holding of a belief of that religion and its manifestation on a non-comparative basis; someone complaining of a breach of freedom of religion does not need to complain that someone else has been treated more favourably.

There is a way of thinking about a second difference between freedom of religion and religious anti-discrimination approaches by using an analogy drawn from sexual orientation. There has long been an important debate within the community of gay activists in Europe, as well as elsewhere, as to the appropriate strategy to adopt in addressing the treatment suffered by those who are gay. Essentially, the alternatives were whether to adopt a strategy based on an argument from privacy, or one based on equality.

In the early days of gay legal activism, the argument from privacy was highly successful in challenging the criminalization of sexual practices, particularly those associated with male homosexuality, such as sodomy. The essence of the argument from privacy was that this right protected activities within a zone of sexual intimacy from state regulation because what one did within that zone of sexual intimacy was, quite simply, not the law's business. The advantage from an activist's perspective was that (conservative) judges were not called on to approve what was done within that zone of privacy, simply tolerate it. This tolerance was based on the need to recognize the desirability of protecting the free choices of autonomous individuals within the zone of sexual intimacy.

The perceived *disadvantage* of the argument from privacy for gay activists was that it appeared to provide very little opportunity to challenge other restrictions on gays and lesbians successfully (other than those on same-sex sexual conduct, that is). After the initial success of the privacy strategy in striking down criminal sodomy laws, the privacy strategy was considered by many to be too limited in what it could be used to achieve. Even more importantly, however, it was not just limit*ed*, but also limit*ing*, in that it appeared to conceptualize the relationship between gays and the wider society only in terms of sexual intimacy, and only in terms of protecting conduct rather than status. Once gays came out of the closet, into the public domain, into the light, then the privacy argument had very little purchase: privacy did not protect homosexuals from being treated badly, it only protected particular actions associated with homosexuals from being penalized (provided they were in private).

The alternative approach that came to dominate gay rights litigation was based on discrimination and equality rather than privacy. A shift to equality would mean that gay activists would no longer have to focus on the particular substantive right of privacy as the basis for challenging particular treatment, but instead would concentrate on the use of the 'status' of sexual orientation, similar to the way in which the use of race or gender or disability came to be seen. This shift to equality was considered to be attractive, in short, because it provided an opportunity to focus on homosexual status rather than homosexual sexual practices alone; it protected gays in the public sphere (as opposed to only in the bedroom) and, because it was based on a conception of discrimination that was comparative, it emphasized, on every occasion, that the starting point for analysis was that homosexuals and non-homosexuals should be treated as equivalent.

This opportunity to validate rather than just tolerate gays was taken up with enthusiasm by gay activists, leading to considerable advances in the perception of homosexuals, who were reclassified (as it were) to become a group worthy of protection, in ways very similar to women, racial minorities, and so on. In this sense,

Justice Scalia was correct in *Romer* v. *Evans* when he said: 'Quite understandably, they [meaning gay activists] devote ... political power to achieving ... not merely a grudging social toleration, but full social acceptance, of homosexuality.' Quoting Jacobs, he considered '[t]he task of gay rights proponents is to move the center of public discourse along a continuum from the rhetoric of disapprobation, to rhetoric of tolerance, and finally to affirmation'. Adopting equality as the basis for its legal strategy contributed to this goal. 'Affirmation' means that these particular choices are not just accepted, but are also regarded as 'right', such that we cannot reject them, and the state (through the courts) is seen to prefer that view over a contesting view.

How is this diversion into the history of gay rights relevant for an analysis of claims to *religious* discrimination? A significant part of the appeal for litigants in using an argument based on freedom from religious discrimination is the opportunity it offers to benefit from similar affirmation of their status as religious persons, particularly when they operate in the public sphere, broadly defined. The opportunity to secure affirmation is notoriously more limited using freedom of religion. Not only is there an ambiguity as to whether the courts will apply a narrow 'autonomy' approach, significantly limiting religion to the private sphere, there is also a focus on particular 'conduct', i.e. the manifestation of a set of religious practices, rather than a protection of the status of being religious in the much broader range of circumstances covered by anti-discrimination law.

Grounds of protection in anti-discrimination law

While the benefits for conscientious-believer litigants appear to be clear, there remains a significant problem. This is the problem of how far, if at all, courts are willing to see religion as truly analogous to other grounds that they regard as appropriately protected by anti-discrimination law, such as race, or gender, or sexual orientation. This requires us to consider the second problem in understanding the *telos* of freedom from religious discrimination. Trying to explain why some grounds are included within the protectorate of anti-discrimination law, while others are not, has generated a substantial debate in different jurisdictions, one that is by no means over.

Initially, the predominant academic explanation in several jurisdictions outside the United States followed that adopted by the US Supreme Court: the common element that linked those grounds that were protected by anti-discrimination law, and that distinguished these from other grounds that were not protected, was said to be that the grounds that were included in the protectorate were all 'immutable characteristics', meaning that these characteristics were not chosen and could not be altered by an individual. In 1969, the *Harvard Law Review* observed that 'race and lineage are congenital and unalterable traits over which an individual has no control and for which he should receive neither blame nor reward'.

The immutability theory has important implications for how we are likely to view the inclusion of 'religion' in the grounds of protection, because it radically distinguishes racial discrimination from much religious discrimination. Whereas the latter is thought to protect individuals because they act on the basis of freely made choices, the former protects individuals because they were acted upon on the basis of characteristics that were not freely chosen. It is this distinction that surfaced some years ago in the British courts, when Lord Justice Sedley in *Eweida* v. *British Airways* distinguished protection from discrimination on the grounds of age, disability, gender reassignment, marriage and civil partnership, race, sex, and sexual orientation, from protection from discrimination on grounds of religion or belief. He observed: 'One cannot help observing that all of these apart from religion or belief are objective characteristics of individuals: *religion and belief alone are matters of choice.*'

In the place of its birth, the 'immutability' theory has, however, long been regarded sceptically, as being both under- and over-inclusive. Lawrence Tribe's comment demonstrates how it is *over*-inclusive: 'Intelligence, height, and strength are all immutable for a particular individual but legislation that distinguishes on the basis of these criteria is not generally thought to be constitutionally suspect.' Jack Balkin's analysis points to why it is *under*-inclusive:

> Discrimination against blacks ... is not unjust simply because race is an immutable characteristic. Focusing on immutability per se confuses

biological with sociological considerations. It confuses the physical existence of the trait with what the trait means in a social system ... The question is not whether a trait is immutable, but whether there has been a history of using the trait to create a system of social meanings, or define a social hierarchy, that helps dominate and oppress people. Any conclusions about the importance of immutability already presuppose a view about background social structure.

Attempting to isolate a principled reason why some groups are protected from being discriminated against and others not brings us face to face with a major unresolved issue in anti-discrimination law theory: what is it that anti-discrimination law is attempting to do? While the 'immutability' theory has lost support, there has been no single alternative that has emerged as a commonly accepted replacement, at least in the European context. Instead, several competing theories have attempted to answer this question.

One theory is that the protected characteristics comprise a list of those characteristics that are irrelevant to the performance of a job, or to the distribution of a benefit, and therefore the use of these characteristics should be prohibited in these contexts. This approach focuses on the function of anti-discrimination law in eradicating irrational decision making, and requiring decision makers to act on the basis of 'merit'. This explanation has always carried a powerful punch, because protection from discrimination on this basis is not just for the benefit of the individual who is protected, but it is also in the general interest that only relevant criteria should be adopted. And, in the context of religion, we can also see that this approach has considerable resonance—it is, in some contexts, simply irrelevant what a person's beliefs (religious or not) are. To this extent, there is a clear overlap between the concern to protect freedom of religion and the concern to prohibit discrimination on religious grounds: both are concerned with preventing others (the state, an employer) from messing with a person's set of beliefs unless this is absolutely necessary. In this theory, whether or not the protected characteristic was the result of free choice by the 'victim' was not important; rather, what was important was the relevance of the criterion to the choice made by the decision maker.

The argument from irrelevance is not, however, particularly convincing if it is presented as a complete explanation for the inclusion on the list of protected characteristics usually covered, not least because in some cases the use of a protected characteristic *is* highly relevant but is still prohibited (think of the prohibition of some actuarial calculations based on gender of pension contributions under European Union law). In the context of the prohibition of religious discrimination, the 'irrelevance' theory is also unconvincing as an all-encompassing explanation, because religious discrimination is prohibited in employment even where it is 'relevant', such as where an employer is prohibited from discriminating against a person on grounds of his or her religion even where the employer's customers would strongly prefer not to have a person of that religion serving them. For the employer to take the employee's religion into account in deciding whether to hire that person could not be described as 'irrational', or based on 'irrelevant' considerations. We prohibit the employer from so acting *in spite of* its being relevant in some circumstances.

Of the alternatives to the 'irrelevance' theory, two others have proved of particular importance. Both of these involve, to some degree, a collective dimension. When the paradigmatic grounds of anti-discrimination law were race and gender, the most popular alternative theory was probably one based on 'redistribution' to particular disadvantaged groups. This theory captured the idea that the function of anti-discrimination law was a modest redistribution of opportunities for employment, housing, and other benefits from advantaged to disadvantaged groups. The source of the disadvantage was clear—it was the race or the gender of the person—and therefore it was appropriate to prohibit the use of those characteristics that would result in these groups being even more disadvantaged. Owen Fiss termed this approach, the 'group disadvantaging principle'. This principle, and its similar cousins, concentrated on the disadvantage (often economic) that the group suffered or would suffer, and associated that disadvantage with the fact that the group was identified by its possession of the prohibited characteristic.

The 'group disadvantaging principle' explains the inclusion of religion in Europe only to a limited extent. So, in Northern Ireland, where religion plays a social role equivalent to ethnicity and there was a significant connection between being Catholic and being disadvantaged, the group-disadvantaging principle explains and justifies the inclusion of religion in anti-discrimination law. So, too, where there is a strong connection elsewhere between ethnicity, religion, and economic disadvantage, such as we see as regards the position of Muslims in Britain, prohibiting religious discrimination seems to map neatly onto the group disadvantaging principle. Except in these contexts, however, the redistributive approach seems singularly ill-suited to explain the inclusion of 'religion' as a *general* category of prohibited characteristic.

A more recent theory, and probably the most popular currently, is the theory of protection based on the desirability of protecting 'minority identity'. Unlike the 'group disadvantaging principle', this seeks to explain the categories of protected characteristics by focusing on the importance of protecting social groups with which individuals self-identify and of which they behave as a part, adopting the shared attitudes and practices of the group to such an extent that their membership in the group becomes an important part of how they view themselves. Such identities should be protected, it is said, because discrimination on the basis of this identity is an attack on a central aspect of the personality of those whose self-identity is tied up with the group. Not all identities are protected, of course, only those that are particularly associated with a 'minority' group, with 'minority' in this context often being a proxy for 'those who are *disadvantaged* as a result of their minority status'.

This theory seems particularly well suited to the inclusion of grounds such as sexual orientation within the protectorate of anti-discrimination law. The legal move from using privacy to using equality arguments in the context of sexual orientation coincided with a social movement that increasingly saw sexual orientation as an identity rather than simply as a description of sexual conduct. The development of sexual orientation as a mark of identity made it that much easier to incorporate it as a protected ground of discrimination. With that move, the issue ceased to be whether sexual orientation was chosen or not, or whether sexual orientation was an 'immutable characteristic' or not. And it was clear that the group was a 'minority', whose members were disadvantaged by being part of that group. Such an approach is not entirely absent from the jurisprudence of the ECtHR. We have seen earlier that the ECtHR, when considering freedom of religion, accepts the connection between religion and identity. Protecting religious choices is seen as important not only because we respect autonomy, but also because these choices relate to the individual's identity. So far, however, the identity-based approach has not been extensively tested in the ECtHR as an appropriate interpretation of Article 14's prohibition of religious discrimination, and its likely adoption by the Court is uncertain.

If the interpretation by British courts of prohibitions on religious discrimination is any basis for predicting future trends elsewhere, including in the ECtHR, equality norms in the context of religion will be seen, rather, as simply another way of putting the freedom of religion approach into practice, and therefore as something of an anomaly in the equality law sphere. So, in recent British cases the anti-discrimination provisions dealing with religion have been interpreted as encapsulating a choice-based approach borrowed directly from freedom of religion rather than an identity-based approach borrowed from race cases. So too, the provisions are interpreted as encapsulating a view that religion is a private matter rather than a public matter, again borrowing directly from freedom of religion; and as focused on conduct rather than identity, again borrowed directly from freedom of religion. What seems to emerge from what is, admittedly, still a somewhat patchy jurisprudence is an approach that seeks to distance religious equality from all the other types of status equality, and to relegate religious equality to become simply another variant of freedom of religion, and therefore subject to the same type of constraints as freedom of religion.

This emerging approach, if such it is, seems to be due in part to the structure of Article 14 itself. Article 14 is parasitic on other Convention rights, meaning that the Court has determined that Article 14 does not come into play unless the case raises an issue that is at least 'within the ambit' of another Convention right. The early jurisprudence of the ECtHR generally viewed the function of Article 14 as peripheral and subsidiary to the other substantive rights. Indeed, the Court in this early phase seems to have regarded the role of Article 14 as essentially a way of ensuring that the fundamental right in issue was more widely distributed, rather than being important in its own right. This is an important reason why, in so many early cases, an Article 14 claim was not decided on its merits after it was found that another substantive right had been breached—Article 14 was not thought to bring anything additional to the table. In the context of litigation involving a claim of religious discrimination, a classic move was to argue that the case raised issues within the ambit of Article 9 on freedom of religion, rather than some other Article, and thus the scene was set for Article 9 to become the dominant focus of attention, replacing the Article 14 discrimination issue.

The approach that regards Article 14 as subsidiary and peripheral has more recently been significantly modified, and eradicating certain types of status inequality is often now seen as a worthy goal in itself. This approach has come to dominate the adjudication of claims based on race, gender, and sexual orientation. These grounds (and some others) are considered by the Court to merit a particularly high degree of protection because adverse treatment based on these grounds is thought to merit particular condemnation. In these cases, the function of Article 14 is not to act as merely ancillary to the other substantive rights but to take on a role in protecting individuals from particular types of status discrimination. When engaging with discrimination on these grounds, the Court now interprets Article 14 in ways much more similar to the classic statutory anti-discrimination law provisions in domestic law, such as those prohibiting racial and gender discrimination.

And, again, this approach is not absent from Article 14 jurisprudence engaging with religious discrimination. The Court has interpreted Article 14 read with Article 9 in somewhat similar ways, in particular where it would appear from the facts of the case that the power of the state was being used to allow one religion to dominate another. Thus, the well-known prejudice against non-Orthodox churches in Greece, and Jehovah's Witnesses more generally, has led the Court to identify these religions as, effectively, 'minorities' and thus subject to greater protection. In these contexts, where heightened scrutiny is required, the Court is also more likely to impose a positive obligation on the state to protect these minority religions from non-state actors, and impose an obligation of reasonable accommodation on the state. However, where the Court does not view the religious anti-discrimination claim as involving, in effect, a claim to disadvantaged minority group status, the Court does not appear to be willing to grant the claimant membership of a 'suspect category', and is anxious to allow to states a wide margin of appreciation. The Court's approach, therefore, is very context driven. That is why we have cases such as *Ladele*, in which the Court appears to understand the *telos* of the religious discrimination provision as the same (or very similar) to that of freedom of religion and thus, crucially, to bring similar limitations into anti-discrimination law as occur in freedom of religion.

Why the unease in applying a straightforward anti-discrimination approach? Two possibilities come to mind. First, the unacceptability of some religious beliefs might be thought to be sufficient in itself to distinguish the ground of 'religion and belief' from other protected characteristics, and this may lead courts to push religious discrimination claims back to the safer shores of freedom of religion where there is more experience of dealing with bigoted religions. Gwyneth Pitt, for example, argues that unlike other protected grounds, which 'express a consensus about particular values of equality and the irrelevance of certain characteristics', the protection of religion and belief 'potentially provides protection for the holders of completely abhorrent, or irrational, or bigoted beliefs, including those which would certainly not accord equal rights to others if they were to prevail', and that this 'highlights a difference between the religion or belief ground compared with other protected grounds'.

Courts may interpret the prohibitions on religious discrimination in what they consider to be a very different context from that in which they interpret the laws prohibiting racial or gender discrimination. Up to this point, they have become used to seeing religious discrimination primarily in an ethnic minority context, and seem to have considerable difficulty in accepting that religious identity is a status that is to be protected irrespective of whether that religious identity is connected with a minority ethnic identity or not. In addition, even when the religious discrimination claim does arise from a community that is a minority ethnic community, the claim to protection is met with a post-multicultural scepticism, particularly where any whiff of illiberalism in the religious practices of that group is perceived to be operating.

If this is what is going on, then it would seem that, in the long run, the language and claims of non-discrimination and equality may be of greater harm than help to religious claimants. Equality language and anti-discrimination claims bear the impression of certain core progressive commitments that do not sit at all easily with the views of some religious believers. But it is contrary to the state's (and the Court's) duty of neutrality and impartiality to allow the state (or the Court) to assess the legitimacy of a system of religious beliefs, or the way in which those beliefs are expressed, and the Court is more likely to prefer dealing with the problem in another way, such as viewing the claim through the narrower lens of freedom of religion.

A second possible explanation for the unease in treating religious discrimination claims as on a par with claims of discrimination on other grounds (except where such claims are closely related to racial and ethnic discrimination) may be because of the wider implications of doing so. Perhaps sensing that they are likely to get into highly problematic water if religious discrimination litigation becomes widespread, the ECtHR has avoided these future problems by invoking the margin of appreciation, thus leaving the issue to the national authorities. The Grand Chamber adopted that approach in *Lautsi*, the case dealing with the display of the crucifix in Italian public school classrooms. One way of interpreting such decisions is to view the Court as according to European states considerable discretion to weigh religious values according to their own criteria of evaluation, thus giving discretion to states also as to how to deal with the problem, and allowing the Court in particular to avoid dealing with the highly sensitive issue of established (or quasi-established) religions.

While this approach may satisfy those concerned with protecting national sovereignty, it does little to address other understandings of why religion should be protected since it places the *state* in the driving seat, allowing it to decide which, if any, religious values to uphold. It seems, if anything, a throwback to the original approach to freedom of religion adopted in the Treaty of Westphalia, in which princes got to determine the religion of the populace in their territories. So, for example, the ECtHR's use of the margin of appreciation to address issues concerned with abortion, or the wearing of Islamic dress, or conscientious objection to same-sex relationships, recognizes the diversity of the values upheld in different *national* traditions. As the ECtHR stated in the *Leyla Şahin* case, concerning the wearing of Islamic dress: 'Rules in this sphere will consequently vary from one country to another according to *national* traditions and the requirements imposed by the need to protect the rights and freedoms of others and so maintain public order … Accordingly, the choice of the extent and form such regulation should take must inevitably be left up to a point to *the State* concerned, as it will depend on the specific domestic context.' But this does little to ensure that human rights norms will protect 'religious values' that a state does not value. And, with some notable exceptions, the theoretical literature emanating from anti-discrimination scholars has been unsympathetic to the dilemmas and inconsistencies this generates, distorted as it sometimes is by a lack of sympathy for religious thought in this secular scholarship. This has led to a lack of theoretical progress, a kind of politico-theoretical deadlock, which has muddled our thinking on both anti-discrimination law and religion.

★★★

We end this chapter where we began with no clearer an idea of what each of these provisions is for. But there are significant differences between how the teleological problem affects the two sets of provisions. In the case of freedom of religion, we find a plethora of justifications that aim to collapse the distinction between freedom of religion and other human rights. In particular, freedom of religion 'becomes' privacy, or freedom of assembly. In the case of freedom from religious discrimination, the problem is rather the opposite: to deny the analogy between religious discrimination and other types of discrimination, and to regard religion as *sui generis*. It is all very confusing.

5

THE EPISTEMOLOGICAL PROBLEM

In this chapter, I consider the second major problem that dominates religious litigation, what I have called the epistemological problem. I identified this earlier as the problem of how we are to understand normative systems other than those to which we are ourselves committed. The particular problem that is the focus of my concern is how those involved in legal interpretation, such as judges, can understand a religious system sufficiently to be able to adjudicate when conflicts arise that depend on an understanding of that other normative system.

Until recently, western legal systems, and English law is an example of this, were thought to embody a principle of abstention when religious issues were raised. In several judicial decisions in the recent past, the courts expressed a strong view that these issues were beyond their competence and authority. It was thought to be a basic principle of law in many countries that the courts would not seek to adjudicate contested questions of religion. One of the noticeable changes in the last few years, however, has been the extent to which that previous reticence has now been replaced with a much more self-confident willingness to decide contested issues touching on the religious sphere, and to do this in ways that require an understanding of the religion in question. In this chapter, after examining the older avoidance strategies, we will consider some of the multiple newer strategies that courts have adopted to enable them to handle the epistemological problem.

AVOIDANCE STRATEGIES

One response by courts is simply to sidestep the problem. Sometimes—indeed, usually, perhaps—courts may stay out of religious controversies out of self-interest, as well as for the sake of the religions concerned. This is one way of viewing what

Litigating Religions: An Essay on Human Rights, Courts, and Beliefs. Christopher McCrudden. © Christopher McCrudden 2018. Published 2018 by Oxford University Press.

the Grand Chamber was doing in *Lautsi*, where the Court said that it was not going to be drawn into the business of conclusively determining the meaning of the crucifix in Italian classrooms. *Hosanna-Tabor* may also be read in much the same way. The Supreme Court in effect said that it is beyond its zone of competence to make *bright-line* rules about who is and who is not a minister of religion. But, even here, the Court does not render the issue entirely beyond its institutional authority or jurisdiction. Rather it says, quite modestly, that *in this case* there *is* enough evidence to conclude that the petitioner was a minister.

A similar approach is what the European Court of Human Rights (ECtHR) calls the 'margin of appreciation'. The handling of the *Ladele* case in the ECtHR provides a good example. The Court held that Article 14 was engaged, and that the public authority's treatment of Ms Ladele amounted to a prima facie breach of Article 14. The principal issue was justification: whether the treatment afforded to Ms Ladele pursued a legitimate aim and was proportionate to the achievement of the aim pursued. The Court held: 'The Court generally allows the national authorities a wide margin of appreciation when it comes to striking a balance between competing Convention rights ... In all the circumstances, the Court does not consider that the national authorities, that is the local authority employer which brought the disciplinary proceedings and also the domestic courts which rejected the applicant's discrimination claim, exceeded the margin of appreciation available to them.'

What is sauce for the goose is sauce for the gander, and the margin of appreciation can also be used to uphold religious values. The Grand Chamber ultimately adopted this approach in *Lautsi*. In both cases, this meant that the Court spared itself from having to consider the meaning of the religion in question, because it avoided having to apply a proportionality approach. One way of interpreting these decisions is to view the ECtHR as according to European states discretion to weigh religious values according to their own criteria of evaluation, thus handing back to these states themselves the question of how best to deal with the epistemological problem. We considered some of the implications of this approach, and the problems it gives rise to more generally, in the previous chapter.

There is an additional avoidance strategy, which is when the court says that the issue in the case is not really about religion at all, but about something else that the court feels more comfortable in dealing with, such as ethnicity. Let's take the *JFS* case as an example. The school sought to make a distinction between two different ways in which someone might be regarded as Jewish, distinguishing between a person being regarded as Jewish in the ethnic sense, and a person being regarded as Jewish in the religious sense. The two were not the same, said the school, and the boy concerned (M) was a perfect example of when the distinction applied. The Office of the Chief Rabbi (OCR) acknowledged that M was 'ethnically' Jewish, in the sense that he self-identified as Jewish, he was significantly involved with the Jewish community in various ways, and he was accepted as Jewish by at least parts of the community. So, if, for example, an anti-Semitic admission's officer at a non-faith based state school refused to admit him because he was Jewish, that should be regarded as prohibited ethnic discrimination because he was being discriminated against on the grounds of his Jewish ethnicity. Although the OCR acknowledged M as 'ethnically Jewish' the OCR did not acknowledge that he was 'religiously Jewish' in the sense determined by *halacha* (Jewish religious law). The school was not, it said, discriminating on the grounds of his ethnicity but on the grounds that he was not of the Jewish religion. Whether he claimed to be an adherent of the Jewish faith, and whether he 'practised' the Jewish faith by going to synagogue and keeping kosher, was irrelevant to whether he was of the Jewish religion, according to Orthodox principles.

The problem for the school, and the key to M's father's case, was that the school's approach emphasized the absence of 'ethnic' *intention* on the part of the OCR. Whereas in the United States, the concept of direct discrimination (disparate treatment) clearly involves an examination into the purpose of the alleged perpetrator's actions, this has been an area of significant debate in the British courts. In an earlier case, the House of Lords held that the test for whether there was direct discrimination, was whether 'but for' the ethnicity of the person, they would have been treated less favourably than they were.

Unsurprisingly, his father argued that 'but for' the fact that the OCR considered that M was not Jewish, he would have been admitted to the school. M argued that the religious test of whether a person was Jewish was in itself an 'ethnic' test because it relied on the idea of descent from the mother, and descent was in itself an ethnic test because it concentrated on a person's origins. The approach taken by the school was to argue that in the JFS context there was no complete overlap between being 'ethnically Jewish' and being 'religiously Jewish'. In identifying the ground on which JFS refused to admit M to the school the Court should adopt a subjective approach that takes account of the motive and intention of JFS, the OCR, and the Chief Rabbi. They were subjectively concerned solely with M's *religious* status, as determined by Jewish religious law. There was no cause to doubt the Chief Rabbi's frankness or good faith on this matter. The availability of conversion demonstrated that the test applied was inherently of a religious rather than racial character. It was inapt to describe the religious dimension of the test being applied by JFS as a mere motive. The appropriate comparator for M in this case is a child whose mother had converted under Orthodox Jewish auspices. The ground of difference in treatment between M and such a child would be that the latter's mother had completed an approved course of Orthodox conversion.

The majority of the Supreme Court, however, held that in determining whether there is direct discrimination on grounds of ethnic origins, the court must determine, *as a question of fact*, whether the victim's ethnic origins is the *factual* criterion that determined the decision made by the discriminator. If so, the motive for the discrimination and the reason why the discriminator considered the victim's ethnic origins significant are irrelevant. Where the factual criteria upon which discriminatory treatment is based are unclear, unconscious, or subject to dispute the court will consider the mental processes of the discriminator in order to infer, as a question of fact from the available evidence, whether there is discrimination on a prohibited ground. It is only necessary, however, to consider the mental processes of the discriminator where the factual criteria underpinning the discrimination are unclear. Direct discrimination does not require that the discriminator intends to behave in a discriminatory manner or that he realizes that he is doing so.

There was, according to the majority, no need, therefore, for any consideration of mental processes of JFS as the factual criterion that determined the refusal to admit M to JFS was clear: the fact that he was not descended in the matrilineal line from a woman recognized by the OCR as Jewish. The subjective state of mind of JFS, the OCR, and the Chief Rabbi was therefore irrelevant. The crucial question to be determined was whether this requirement was properly characterized as referring to M's ethnic origins. The test applied by JFS in fact focused upon the ethnicity of the women from whom M is descended. Whether such women were themselves born as Jews or converted in a manner recognized by the OCR, the only basis upon which M would be deemed to satisfy the test for admission to JFS would be that he was descended in the matrilineal line from a woman recognized by the OCR as Jewish. It was stressed that while it was possible for women to convert to Judaism in a manner recognized by the OCR and thus confer Orthodox Jewish status upon their offspring, the requirement of undergoing such conversion itself constituted a significant and onerous burden that was not applicable to those born with the requisite ethnic origins. This was seen as further illustrating the essentially ethnic nature of the OCR's test. Some of the tricky questions of Jewish religious beliefs could be avoided, therefore, by regarding the issue as one of ethnicity.

EXTERNAL AND INTERNAL POINTS OF VIEW

But courts also, sometimes, do engage directly with the beliefs of a religious person, or a religious community, and they are then confronted directly with the epistemological problem. We can best analyse the variety of differing approaches that courts adopt in addressing this problem by having in mind two distinctions. The first distinction is already familiar from the previous chapter, the distinction between religion conceived collectively and religion conceived as a private, individual belief system. We shall need to keep this in mind during the course of this chapter as well. But there is a second distinction that has not, thus far, been drawn on and we must spend a little time getting to grips with it. This is the distinction between *external and internal* approaches to normative systems of thought. We shall see that the approaches that courts take vary, depending on which of both sets of distinctions the courts ultimately prefer.

When the boy in *Mandla* v. *Dowell-Lee* wanted to wear his turban to a Church of England school, the court decided that wearing a turban was an essential aspect of Sikhism. In practical terms, determining such issues often involves the difficulty of courts deciding what evidence is admissible and probative as to what practices or beliefs of a religion are central. In the *JFS* case, the issue did not concern how central the issue was to the religion concerned (it was common ground that membership of the religion was a central, if deeply contested, aspect of what constituted the Jewish religion), but rather how the court should view the relationship between being Jewish as a matter of ethnicity and being Jewish as a matter of religion. The court considered detailed evidence regarding how the different branches of Judaism defined a person as Jewish, and indeed how the boy at the centre of the dispute himself viewed his relationship to the religion.

Other disciplines have struggled with a similar issue. Historiographical debates, for example, have considered how historians can analyse forms of early religion. One approach is to regard these religions simply from an external viewpoint, as the outward manifestations of forces that the believers themselves may not even have been aware of. So, for example, the approach that Keith Thomas famously adopted in his analysis of religion, drawing from African cultural anthropology, considered religious practices in sixteenth-century England from the point of view of an external observer. Such external, or detached, views may often be appropriate. We might want to look at the external behaviour of those who are religious without necessarily taking their understanding of what they are doing as determinative, just as some sociolegal or law-and-economics scholars consider the behaviour of some legal actors from a similarly external viewpoint. Observing the regularity of behaviour of a group of actors may be useful without looking at what is going on in the minds of those so acting.

It would be a mistake, however, to consider that such an external perspective is the only way to study religious contributions to human rights discourse. More recently, there has been a turn to take more seriously the belief systems of religious believers themselves, and the significance of those beliefs, from their own (internal) perspective. This involves an attempt to understand rather than simply to observe. This internal perspective is also the approach lawyers expect those writing about *law* to take about some legal phenomena. Famously, the legal philosopher H. L. A. Hart distinguished between external and internal points of view in approaching the concept of law. A sophisticated approach to the study of legal doctrine requires the scholar not just to adopt an external perspective, observing the law as a cultural phenomenon involving certain practices, but also as a normative system that requires understanding from an internal perspective.

To capture the internal understanding of the normative system does not require acceptance of these internal beliefs. The reason for this is because there are two types of internal perspective available. Neil MacCormick distinguished between two components of the internal point of view: 'There is [the] "cognitively internal" point of view, from which conduct is appreciated and understood in terms of the standards which are being used by the agent as guiding standards: that is sufficient for an understanding of norms and the normative.' This should be contrasted with what MacCormick terms a 'volitionally internal' point of view, which he characterizes as 'the point of view of an agent, who in some degree and for reasons which seem good to him has a volitional commitment to observance of a given pattern of conduct as a standard for himself or for other people or for both: his attitude includes, but is not included by, the "cognitively internal" attitude'.

Similarly, both courts (and scholars) writing about normative systems that make up particular religions are faced with choices about which is the appropriate approach to adopt in addressing religious claims.

IDENTIFYING A TAXONOMY OF APPROACHES TO ENGAGING WITH RELIGION

We have, therefore, two critical distinctions which come into play: a distinction between understanding religion primarily as a collective enterprise, or as an individual practice; and a distinction between taking an external point of view, or also adopting an internal point of view (and, if so, of what type: cognitive or volitional). Bringing these individual–collective and the external–internal perspectives together, we can begin to identify the various ways in which courts tackle the epistemological problem, combining these perspectives in various different combinations, with some more popular than others.

Volitional commitment by judge

In the past, it was relatively commonplace for judges to declare their personal commitment to a particular religion, and use their personal knowledge of that religion in order to decide what the belief system of that religion involved, effectively taking 'judicial notice' of the beliefs of that religion. In most cases, judges who did so were interpreting the dominant religion of the jurisdiction in which they served as judges: Protestantism in England, Catholicism in Ireland, and so on. For a judge now to adopt this approach in a Western legal system would be shocking. We expect judges not to bring volitional commitment into the courtroom or judges' chambers. This is not to say, however, that such approaches are no longer to be found. In several jurisdictions, judges continue to draw on their (volitionally committed) internal understanding of a religion in their interpretative and adjudicatory roles, as cases in Malaysia and Israel occasionally still evidence.

Individual/internal: religion as a personal belief system

In a second approach, now more common than the first, the courts address the epistemological problem of understanding the claimant's religious engagement by relying on the person's own, volitionally committed, understanding of that belief. This approach attempts to deal with the epistemological problem by constructing religions as essentially *personal* belief systems, and therefore the primary evidence the court needs to be concerned with relates to the beliefs of the single party raising the religious issue. The approach is to investigate only what the individual who claims to act on the basis of his or her own religious beliefs actually believes, irrespective of whether any representative institution to which the individual claims to belong shares the same beliefs or regards them as integral to the religion. This approach emphasizes the 'authenticity' of the individual's own religious experience, concentrating on the meaning and importance of that subjective, individual belief to the person themselves.

A plausible understanding of this development is that, in order to avoid dealing with the epistemic problem of understanding an organized religious belief system, courts embrace an approach to religion that views it, and the protection of freedom of religion, as essentially protecting private and personal choices, rather than protecting the public manifestation of comprehensive belief systems in organized collective religious structures. A prominent example of this approach can be found in the Supreme Court of Canada. In several cases, the majority of the Court has defined what constitutes a 'religion' for the purposes of 'freedom of religion' protected under the Canadian Charter of Rights and Freedoms and the equivalent Quebec Charter in this way. Defined broadly, they said, religion is about 'freely and deeply held *personal* convictions or beliefs connected to an *individual's* spiritual faith and integrally linked to his or her *self-definition* and spiritual fulfilment, the practices of which allow *individuals* to foster a connection with the divine or with the subject or object of that spiritual faith' (emphasis added). For a person's practices and beliefs to be protected under freedom of religion, then, all that an individual need demonstrate initially is that he or she 'sincerely believes' or is 'sincerely undertaking' these practices to 'foster a connection with the divine or with the subject or object of that spiritual faith'.

Personal belief and sincere commitment was all that was necessary, and it was not necessary to show whether a particular practice or belief 'is required by official religious dogma or is in conformity with the position of religious officials'. This understanding was 'consistent with a personal or subjective understanding of freedom of religion'. The person claiming protection 'need not show some sort of objective religious obligation, requirement or precept to invoke freedom of religion'. The essence of the inquiry by the court was initially into the sincerity of the claimant's belief. The court's role is to 'ensure that a presently asserted belief is in good faith, neither fictitious nor capricious, and that it is not an artifice'. Since the focus of the inquiry 'is not on what others view the claimant's religious obligations as being, but rather what the claimant views these personal religious "obligations"' to be, it is inappropriate to require expert opinions to show sincerity of belief'.

External point of view applied to a religion conceived as a collective enterprise

Under a third approach, the court takes the bull by the horns and purports to interpret the religious belief system, understood as a collective enterprise, from an external point of view, although they may describe what they are doing somewhat differently.

Several cases discussed earlier illustrate this approach. In the cases relating to the ability of churches to hire and fire employees, involving the issue of the autonomy of churches and other religiously affiliated entities such as schools and social service organizations in their hiring and personnel decisions, the ECtHR comes perilously close to making determinations about what really lies at the core of different religions from an external point of view—both how important the rules against adultery are to the church, and how important a particular job is to the religious mission of the church. To say, in effect, that Schüth was 'just the organist' ignores the centrality of music to the liturgy and the Mass. Similarly, if the Court were to say, Obst was 'just the PR person', this would discount the centrality of who acts as spokesperson (who gets to speak on behalf of a group).

One other example must suffice for the moment. In *Surayanda*, in which a British Court had to decide whether the destruction of the sacred cow could lawfully proceed, the Court held that there was 'no doubt that [the importance of these religious beliefs and practices] was brought home to the Minister'. But one can legitimately doubt whether that can have been the case. It must surely be the case that if the Minister had believed that the killing of the bullock was really considered by the religion to be equivalent to the killing of a human being, the weight given to that belief would have been greater than it was. In these cases, the court takes what I have called a distinctly 'external' viewpoint, even when it purports to do otherwise.

Court decides the objective 'meaning' of the religious practice using experts

Courts and tribunals faced with the epistemological problem frequently resort to calling expert evidence to enable it to decide between parties disputing which representative or which set of beliefs is authentic from the perspective of the organized religion. Recently, for example, the Charity Commission for England and Wales accepted an application for registration as a charity from the Preston Down Trust (PDT), a Plymouth Brethren Christian Church (PBCC) meeting hall. The Commission had earlier rejected an application for registration by the PDT on the grounds that it was not satisfied it was able to determine conclusively that the doctrines and practices of the PBCC as practised by PDT, but rejected by other Christian congregations, nevertheless met the public benefit requirement in charity law. In deciding to revise its decision, the Commission took into account independent expert evidence as to the nature of the doctrines and religious practices of the Brethren as an organized religious group. In this and similar cases, the purpose in hearing such expert evidence is for the court or tribunal to decide what contested practices involve (and then how acceptable they are).

There are two particular problems with this approach. First, what are the relevant sources? Consider the problem of defining what 'the Catholic' position is. We can identify various sources of what is called the *magisterium* of the Church—that is, the exercise by the Catholic hierarchy, particularly the Pope, of a formal teaching role. In supporting various propositions about what 'Catholic doctrine' requires, all of the following are relevant: the *Catechism of the Catholic Church*, Papal encyclicals, papal homilies and addresses, statements from the Congregation for the Doctrine of the Faith, and Pastoral letters from Bishops. But citing all these sources together to demonstrate 'Catholic doctrine' risks underestimating the hierarchical nature of Church authority, and the way in which the *magisterium* is manifested.

Nor, when the Catholic doctrinal position is being identified is it appropriate to focus only on the *magisterium*. There are, to put it in more traditionally legal terms, three sources of Catholic doctrine in addition to the *magisterium*. These include revelation, natural law, and human experience. This multiplicity of sources means that, taken together, they can be interpreted in a variety of ways that tell different stories about what that religion requires. Perhaps of particular significance, it means that these sources require sophisticated interpretation, and an important source of such interpretation is the works of current theologians. Given that theologians are likely to disagree, the court is then placed in the position of having to decide between the theologians what the doctrine of the Catholic Church is. Is this really the function of a secular court?

Translating religious discourse into 'public reason'

The final approach that is evident when courts engage directly with the interpretation of a religion is to convert the religious language in which the religious believer or the religious group presents their case into a form more consistent with the courts' understanding of what would constitute acceptable reasons, what I'll term a strategy of 'translating' the religious belief in question. Adopting such an approach has the effect of emphasizing the importance of interests being articulated in a form that is consistent with the idea of what has been called 'public reason'. Grégoire Webber explains the concept well. '[A public reason] is a communicative orientation that provides me (a citizen) with a norm against which to evaluate whether my reasons are appropriate in my attempt to convince you (a fellow citizen) of the merits of my argument.' Quoting John Finnis, he continues: 'My reasons should only be those reasons which are "accessible" to all fellow citizens "whatever their religious beliefs or cultural practices" '. It involves a 'willingness' on the part of the citizen, as John Rawls put it 'to listen to others and a fairmindedness in deciding when accommodations to [one's] views should reasonably be made'.

In adopting a translation strategy, the court effectively says to the religious believer: 'what you really mean is . . .', and then translates what the believer has said into more 'acceptable' language, language that conforms to public reason. Perhaps the most explicit example of judicial use of a translation strategy is that adopted in *JFS*. Evidence had been presented on behalf of the Chief Rabbi that explicitly denied the need for any 'conscious affiliation' in Judaism. Indeed, the whole point of the Chief Rabbi's argument was that one could be Jewish according to religious law and explicitly reject any conscious affiliation with the Jewish religion or faith. Yet, in *JFS*, Lord Phillips says this: 'Membership of a religion or faith *normally* indicates some degree of conscious affiliation with the religion or faith on the part of the member' (emphasis added).

The adoption of a 'public reasons' approach addresses the epistemological problem by translating the way the religion formulates its arguments into ways that the court will find understandable (and acceptable) and therefore the epistemological problem does not arise *for the court*. It may, however, arise for the religion, which is then faced with the task of resisting an unacceptable translation, thereby risking losing the court's sympathy, or itself converting its belief system into public reason terms. Those who argue for particular human rights, such as freedom of religion, or who argue for the limits on other rights in the name of freedom of religion, are thus now frequently under a duty to articulate their religious beliefs using such public reasons. To be effective in the judicial context, those involved must be able to conceptualize their argument, and present it, in this form. There may well be tensions, however, between the requirement of 'public reason' in this sense and the discourse which religions consider best expresses their beliefs. The ability to articulate competing interpretations of a particular religious tradition in language that comes closest to 'public reason' affects the likelihood of success or failure.

Faith-based NGOs increasingly regard it as important, more generally, to formulate their arguments in non-religious terms to appeal to other, secular NGOs and secular states. As Berger remarks: 'By choosing to classify themselves as NGOs, religious organizations—consciously or unconsciously—take on a political identity and inject their uniquely religious voices into a predominantly secular discourse about the nature of the new world order.' Given that religious NGOs must cultivate allies among states and other NGOs to make any headway, the language that they use must also appeal to a secular as well as a religious audience, which can sometimes force religious NGOs onto a terrain with which they are neither comfortable nor particularly expert. For Haynes, the need to secure allies among states and secular NGOs has significant effects on the type of language that will be used by such NGOs. It means 'that to be significant players in global public policy debates, they must necessarily adopt and adapt to the terms and rationale of liberal—that is, non-religious—discourse, *even when they do not agree with it*'. As Mahnoush Arsanjani observed in his study of the process of negotiating the UN cloning resolution: 'Perspectives that are unique to a particular religion and lack the same degree of commitment in other religious or nonreligious practices do not easily win international acceptability and priority.'

This partly explains why religious litigation is often conducted in a discourse that is not explicitly religious, and why religious believers increasingly resort to human rights principles other that freedom of religion and religious discrimination, such as freedom of expression, or freedom of association, either alone or together with these rights. The recent example of the *Ashers Bakery* case illustrates the point well. As we shall see in the next chapter, the case was litigated relying heavily on a freedom of expression argument, taken together with freedom of religion. The strategy failed, however, in the Northern Ireland Court of Appeal, when the Court refused to accept the 'translation', holding that there was no substantial difference between a freedom of expression argument and a religious freedom argument, and then proceeded to deal only with the latter, only to dismiss it too. A case, perhaps, of damned if you do and damned if you don't.

6

THE ONTOLOGICAL PROBLEM

We saw in Chapter 4 that different jurisdictions, and even different courts within the same jurisdiction, take very different approaches to the vexed question of what, precisely, the provisions dealing with religion in human and constitutional rights texts are for. When this difficulty is combined with difficulties over how to identify religious belief, we can see clearly that the courts, and litigants, are faced with an uncertain landscape. In Chapter 5, we saw that courts take very different approaches to the equally vexed question of how best to address the difficulty of understanding normative systems other than one's own, and that there are several different approaches in evidence. Some approaches minimize the circumstances in which an independently arrived at internal understanding by the court of the collective religious practice is necessary. In one of these, the court's approach is essentially to delegate to some other body the role of deciding the collective religious practice. In other approaches, the courts 'translate' the religious claim into some other claim, avoiding the religious dimension. Other approaches engage more directly with the religious beliefs, but also demonstrate considerable differences in approach, with some taking an external approach, some an internal. Even those who adopt an internal approach differ significantly.

In this chapter, we explore a third major difficulty in how courts deal with religion in the human rights context. This chapter attempts to grapple with what I have called the ontological problem, but might also be called the 'anthropological problem', by which I mean the problem of what it means to be human. This arises in two particular respects in the relationship between human rights law and religion. The first respect is in the need to give content to the 'human' in 'human rights', and we see religions and legal interpretation giving diverse, and sometimes conflicting,

Litigating Religions: An Essay on Human Rights, Courts, and Beliefs. Christopher McCrudden. Published 2018 by Oxford University Press.

answers to this question. One of the contested sites of this conflict is over how we are to understand the idea of 'human dignity', which is seen by several religions and by the human rights system as a foundational concept for the understanding of human rights. The second respect in which the ontological problem arises has to do with a specific element in what it means to be human, namely the place of religion in that understanding. Is religion central to our view of what it means to be human, and are protections for religion central, therefore, to the human rights enterprise? Or should we, rather, view religion as marginal, or even contrary to our conception of what it means to be fully human, and query whether religion should be part of human rights protections at all?

GIVING CONTENT TO THE 'HUMAN' IN HUMAN RIGHTS

Several of the divergences and tensions between human rights, particularly as interpreted by courts, and religions, are attributable to different approaches to the ontological problem. We can see, for example, that this is the case regarding differences between the human rights and the Catholic traditions regarding the life interest. In the Catholic tradition, foetuses, the mentally incompetent, and those in permanent vegetative states all clearly retain the right to life. This is only partly to do with different conceptions of who can be a rights holder, and much more to do with different meanings and weights attributed to human life in the Catholic tradition, as compared with the legal tradition. This is a significant and recurring issue, and has effects well beyond abortion and euthanasia, in particular in areas relating to biomedical research and treatment, where tensions between the Catholic and legal positions are clearly apparent.

A good example of the conflict this can engender not only between human rights and organized religion, but also between one religion and another is seen in the adoption of the UN cloning resolution. In December 2001, the United Nations General Assembly began considering an international convention against the reproductive cloning of humans. Several states, strongly supported by the Holy See and a raft of religiously affiliated NGOs, took the opportunity provided by this debate to urge a prohibition not only of reproductive cloning, but also of all forms of human cloning which they considered to violate human dignity. An international convention to prohibit such cloning was proposed but, unable to reach a consensus on a binding convention, and opposed by Organisation of Islamic Cooperation, whose members were 'unprepared to support a position so closely associated with Catholic religious teaching', a non-binding and somewhat ambiguous Declaration on Human Cloning was adopted in March 2005.

So, too, there is a clear difference between the human rights and the Catholic traditions in the relationship between the individual and the community. The Catholic claim that human beings are *by nature* social beings, 'made for life together in a universal community', has several important implications, but particularly in the relationship between rights and duties. In the human rights context, we often think of the right as *giving rise* to the duty or obligation. The Catholic tradition appears to reverse the traditional relationship in legal thinking, with the right *following from* the duty or obligation. Rights are more heavily conceptualized in Catholic thought as properly situated, David Hollenbach reminds us, within a communitarian perspective. Rights exist to further the 'common good'. We might conceptualize this in terms of the interest each of us has to further the common good, but it is probably more accurate to see the individual in the Catholic tradition as only fully human when according others what is due to them.

As we have seen in the previous chapter, aspects of Catholic thought are also sometimes in considerable tension with emerging equality norms, which have become central to human rights thinking. Catholic anthropology creates a considerable barrier between Catholic and some legal understandings of women's rights. There appears to be some deep anxiety surrounding this issue deriving from Catholic anthropology, in particular the idea of the complementarity of men and women. The Catechism, for example, states that 'God gives man and woman an equal personal dignity' but also that the harmony of society 'depends in part on the way in which the complementarity, needs, and mutual support between the sexes are lived out'. Discrimination against women in the workplace is seen as 'offensive to the dignity ... of women', but this offence seems to be based on a view that the 'feminine genius is needed in all expressions in the life of society'. Removing gender discrimination is thus seen as necessary, but it is necessary in order to take into account the 'vocation of women', which is likely to send alarm bells ringing, given the secular human rights scepticism of women having a 'vocation' specific to women. So, too, when dealing with women's equality at work, the Catechism also relies on a somewhat essentialist view of women. Work should be restructured 'in such a way that women do not have to pay for their advancement by abandoning what is specific to them'.

What all this means in practice is deeply contested but often appears pretty suspicious to many who advocate the human rights of women. It also has deep implications, of course, for the debate over LGBT rights, and particularly the legal recognition of same-sex marriage. The Congregation for the Doctrine of the Faith's 2003 statement opposing same-sex marriage begins with the statement that 'Men and women are equal as persons and complementary as male and female.'

HUMAN DIGNITY

One of the contested sites of this conflict is over how we are to understand the idea of 'human dignity', which is seen by several religions but also by the human rights system as a foundational concept for the understanding of human rights. I suggested in a previous article that it is possible to discern a certain family resemblance between differing ways of viewing human dignity. In this family resemblance, it was suggested, we can, perhaps, see the outlines of a basic minimum content of 'human dignity'. In this chapter, I draw on that earlier discussion, but develop and modify it somewhat. This basic minimum content seems to me to have at least three elements.

The first element, quoting David Sulmasy, is that human dignity expresses 'that worth or value that people have simply because they are human'. For Sulmasy, this conception of dignity is itself dependent on the concept of 'intrinsic value', which is 'the value something has of itself—the value it has by virtue of its being the kind of thing that it is'. Intrinsic dignity, then, is 'the name we give to the special kind of intrinsic value that belongs to members of natural kinds that have kind-specific capacities'. Recognizing the intrinsic value of something 'depends upon one's ability to discern what kind of thing it is' which involves a 'modest essentialism', that is, it involves the identification of the 'essence' of the thing, 'that by which one picks it out from the rest of reality as anything at all—its being a member of a kind'. This first element is what might be called the 'intrinsic' claim.

The second element in the minimum core is that human dignity should be recognized and respected by others, and some forms of treatment by others are inconsistent with, or required by, human dignity. This second element might be called the 'relational' claim. Human rights discourse since 1945 has gone further and supplemented the relational element of the minimum core by supplying a third element regarding the relationship between the state and the individual. This is the claim that recognizing the human dignity of the individual requires that the state should be seen to exist for the sake of the individual human being, and not vice versa (the limited-state claim).

This concept of human dignity is, of course, stated at a very high level of generality. Even if we accept these three claims, the concept of human dignity holds within it the seeds for much debate and contestation. We can say, on the basis of what we have described up to this point, that while there is a *concept* of human dignity with a minimum core, there are several different *conceptions* of human dignity, and these differ significantly because there appears to be no consensus politically or philosophically on how any of the three claims that make up the core of the concept is best understood. They differ, first, in their understanding of what the intrinsic worth of the individual human being consists in. Conceptions of intrinsic dignity may, for example, be either metaphysical or non-metaphysical. Some argue that the concept of dignity depends on a metaphysical understanding of the human in relation to a *deity*, for example. But there are also non-metaphysical understandings of 'human dignity' that are nevertheless intrinsic, where the dignity of the person is seen to derive from an understanding of what it means to be human, based on our observations of *human experience*.

They also differ in their understanding of what forms of treatment are inconsistent with this worth, and in how this element relates to intrinsic dignity. Sulmasy terms this second element, 'attributed dignity'. Attributed dignity is 'that worth or value that human beings confer upon others by acts of attribution'. He regards this as parasitic (my term, not his) on the idea of intrinsic dignity. This is a controversial move, as we might consider that we can attribute dignity to others without considering that they have intrinsic dignity in the form I have just described.

Finally, they differ in their understanding of the detailed implications of accepting the intrinsic and relational claims for the role of the state vis-à-vis the individual, beyond the core idea that the individual does not exist for the state.

While the role of human dignity, then, is frequently seen as central to explanations of the foundations of human rights, we can identify several understandings of the relationship between dignity and human rights. In one understanding, dignity is seen as providing the basis for human rights in general, in the sense of providing a key argument as to why humans should have rights, and what the limits of these rights may be. In this sense, dignity is the basis for human rights to exist, and there are thinner and thicker variations of this approach. In the thinnest approach, dignity is viewed as simply another way of expressing the idea of a catalogue of human rights. Dignity neither adds to, nor detracts from, rather it is coterminous with human rights and therefore adds little to the debate as to what rights there are, or how they should be interpreted.

Others adopt a somewhat thicker view of dignity seeing it not as a synonym for human rights but rather as expressing a value unique to itself, on which human rights are built. In this thicker use, the role that dignity plays is primarily to help in the identification of a catalogue of specific rights. This catalogue is not closed, however, and the general principle may continue to generate more rights over time as its implications are better understood or changes occur that give rise to new situations that require the application of the general principle for the first time. More generally, however, dignity becomes an interpretative principle to assist the further explication of the catalogue of rights generated by the principle. Some (or all) of the rights, then, come to be seen as best interpreted through the lens of dignity.

THEOLOGIES OF INTRINSIC DIGNITY

We have already seen numerous examples of the use of 'human dignity' as a foundational principle in some religious conceptions of human rights, for example in Catholic social teaching. The concept of dignity should, we might imagine, be shared space between those religions, particularly the Catholic Church, and human rights law, since human dignity is central to religious and secular perspectives on rights. In both, 'human dignity' is often considered to be of fundamental importance for the enterprise. But how far is it the case that they share a similar understanding of the concept of the 'human' in human rights and human dignity?

We have seen that one understanding of intrinsic dignity is that it refers to a particular kind of excellence that each thing has. From this perspective, a lot of different things can be seen as having dignity. *Human* dignity involves recognition of the excellence that persons have, their inherent worth as persons. What is the basis on which such an idea of intrinsic dignity should be based? We can usefully refer to Pope Benedict's theory of human rights at this point. Benedict's response to the question posed was both metaphysical and non-metaphysical. It was metaphysical in emphasizing that human persons are made in the image of God; it is this that makes us special. This is a constant theme: at Westminster, he referred to the 'overriding concern to safeguard the unique dignity of every human person, created in the image and likeness of God'. *Imago Dei* is seen within several religious traditions, in particular, as pointing in the direction of human beings as free and rational. Each and every person has an intrinsic value because of that difference between the human species and other species.

For Jews and Christians, one source of this understanding is revelation, particularly the famous text in Genesis. Unsurprisingly, the Catholic conception of rights is based on a theological understanding. Human rights are important in protecting human dignity in the Catholic tradition, because all human persons share in the divine. For James Hanvey, however, an account based on the account of creation in Genesis presents an impoverished understanding of *imago Dei*. A reading based only on Genesis does not take sufficiently into account the very substantial change in our understanding of *imago Dei*, rooted in Christian tradition, which links the idea of *imago Dei* with the idea of the Trinity, that is the idea that God is three 'persons' in unity. If one believes that God is Trinity, then in what sense are humans, created in the image of God, also Trinitarian? For Hanvey, in contemplating and reflecting on the nature of the 'persons' in the Trinity, the concepts of reciprocity, mutuality, and equality can all be derived, thus contributing significantly to a richer understanding of human dignity. The human person is not a *representative* of God, or a carrier of God's holiness; the human person from the Christian perspective is already endowed with dignity, already possessing that image which cannot be destroyed, or removed, or taken away. It can be debased, it can be effaced; but it cannot be lost, and this, according to Hanvey, carries a strong ontological meaning.

This is nicely captured in the American Bishops' statement *Economic Justice for All*, when, quoting Genesis, it suggests that: 'When we deal with each other, we should do so with the sense of awe that arises in the presence of something holy and sacred. For that is what human beings are: we are created in the image of God (Genesis 1:27).' It then proceeds to go beyond Genesis. This specialness not only derives from the human person being made in the image of God, however, but also because of the implications of Christ's death and resurrection: '[A]ll of the Church's work in pursuit of both justice and peace is designed to protect and promote the dignity of every person. For each person not only reflects God, but is the expression of God's creative work and the meaning of Christ's redemptive ministry.' There is, then, a crucial transcendent dimension to what it means to be 'human' that has important implications for how we treat other persons.

However, Catholic human rights theory, based on human dignity, is at the same time non-metaphysical, emphasizing that human dignity is also based on an anthropological understanding of what it is to be human and that this is derived from human reasoning, reflecting on experience. At the Bundestag, Benedict stressed the importance of reason and nature. 'Christian theologians', he said, 'aligned themselves ... on the side of philosophy, and ... acknowledged reason and nature in their interrelation as the universally valid source of law'. He returned to this theme even more explicitly at Westminster: 'The Catholic tradition maintains that the objective norms governing right action are accessible to reason, prescinding from [i.e. leaving out of consideration] the content of revelation.' There is no conflict between the metaphysical and non-metaphysical approaches because 'not to act in accordance with reason is contrary to God's nature' and so being created in the image of God requires the exercise of reason.

The approach reflected here has been termed 'Christian personalism' or Thomistic personalism, and is associated with French Catholic debates during the interwar period, in particular those involving Jacques Maritain. Thomas Williams has identified the core of personalism as a school of thought or an intellectual movement that 'focuses on the reality of the person ... and on his unique dignity, insisting on the radical distinction between persons and all other beings (nonpersons)'. Williams sets out the distinctive characteristics of personalism as including also 'a concern for the person's subjectivity, attention to the person as object of human action to be treated as an end and never as a mere means, and particular regard for the social (relational) nature of the person'. Personalism, therefore, has been viewed not only as an important influence in strengthening the use of the concept of dignity within Catholicism but also, via Maritain, in contributing to the development of the Universal Declaration on Human Rights, in particular its emphasis on human dignity.

Human dignity, in this tradition, is an intrinsically valuable status possessed by all human beings simply in virtue of their humanity, and discoverable by ordinary moral reasoning or through natural reason. Human rights concern those rights that persons have simply in virtue of their humanity. In the Catholic tradition, then, 'human dignity' provides the core underpinning of human rights. *Pacem in Terris* stated: 'Any human society, if it is to be well-ordered and productive, must lay down as a foundation this principle, namely, that every human being is a person, that is, his nature is endowed with intelligence and free will. Indeed, precisely because he is a person he has rights and obligations flowing directly and simultaneously from his very nature.' And the consequences of persons having dignity overlap with several secular (particularly Kantian) understandings: '[T]he Christian basis of any theory of human rights', the Pontifical Commission has written, 'is respect for the human person as an end in himself, not as a social instrument'.

This approach has several significant implications, which we shall come to in due course. One implication is that it emphasizes, and supports, the universality of human rights, because they are grounded in the dignity of the human person, which is itself a universal idea. The rights recognized and expounded in the Universal Declaration of Human Rights, Benedict insisted, 'apply to everyone by virtue of the common origin of the person ... They are based on the natural law inscribed on human hearts and present in different cultures and civilizations ... This great variety of viewpoints must not be allowed to obscure the fact that not only rights are universal, but so too is the human person, the subject of those rights.' Not to base human rights on the secure foundations of the human person was to risk relativism and the destruction of the universality of human rights: 'Removing human rights from this context would mean restricting their range and yielding to a relativistic conception, according to which the meaning and interpretation of rights could vary and their universality would be denied in the name of different cultural, political, social and even religious outlooks.'

SCEPTICISM CONCERNING INTRINSIC DIGNITY

Courts interpreting human rights principles and adjudicating human rights claims use the rhetoric of human dignity frequently. They seldom analyse what it means, however, and I have never come across a judicial discussion that engages seriously with the question whether, and how far, the judicial use of the discourse of human dignity is consistent with (any or some) religious uses of the term. A close analysis of the practice of the courts, however, suggests that, were they to articulate their understanding of human dignity, many courts would reject, for example, the intrinsic understanding of human dignity that I have attributed to Catholic theology.

The scepticism that I attribute to the courts is reconstructed from practice. It seems to me to overlap with the scepticism of some recent philosophers' discussion of intrinsic human dignity. One objection to the idea of 'intrinsic dignity' is that 'the intrinsic claim' might be thought to involve a controversial (because non-secular) claim about persons. Deriving human dignity from the Image of God clearly encounters this problem. For Sergio Dellavalle the principal disadvantage of *imago Dei* is its close relationship with religion and its resulting parochialism: an idea of dignity based on this understanding is accessible only to the adherents of a religious group, and seems to exclude others. It would be difficult to imagine any of the courts we have considered so far in this essay consistently adopting *imago Dei* as the basis for its understanding of human rights.

We have seen, however, that there are 'secular' understandings of intrinsic dignity. Do they also encounter the same problem? Michael Rosen, in his book on human dignity, attributes the rise of human dignity as the foundation for the universal entitlement to human rights to the coming together after the Second World War of two powerful traditions: Christian theology and Kantian philosophy. In the Christian tradition, the human person has dignity because that person is made in the image of God; in the Kantian tradition, according to Rosen, '[h]uman beings have dignity because the moral law, the unique intrinsically and unconditionally valuable thing that there is, is embodied in us and in us alone'. Both, though in different ways (one religious, the other purportedly not), view the human person as uniquely valuable, possessing an 'inner transcendental kernel' that is embodied in all of us, a core of value that must be protected.

Adopting a specifically Christian understanding of dignity would, of course, be problematic in a liberal, pluralistic constitutional tradition, but why not a Kantian conception? We see some courts, particularly in Germany, doing just that and, when they do, the discourse, and the implications of dignity, can closely mirror religious understandings of dignity. For some, however, that is part of the problem. Rosen, for example, considers that adopting Kant's understanding of dignity is equally problematic, and for the same reason. Although, Rosen argues, Kant's theory is 'independent of belief in God', yet his moral philosophy 'with its emphasis on the "inviolable holiness" of humanity and the primacy of respect ... for humanity in our persons turns out to be far from fully secular'.

Much of the recent philosophical literature exploring the concept of human dignity, and I suggest (more silently) the practice of the courts, has sought to distance itself from intrinsic dignity for another reason. For those who want to use the conception of human dignity that identifies an 'inner kernel' of value or worth, the problem is how to do so in a way that can appeal to public reason, and is not dependent on a religious or quasi-religious understanding of the person that is unacceptable in human rights terms. Tollefsen, for example, considers that a capacities-based approach establishes the basis for intrinsic dignity in this sense. However, as Emily Jackson argued, if humans are special because of their special characteristics, then what are the implications? Animals like dolphins, whales, and the great apes share some of those special characteristics, whereas persistently vegetative human beings do not. Why are the lives of animals not also in some sense sacred? As soon as we identify a particular capacity of the human being as that which confers intrinsic value or dignity, its absence in a particular individual can then be taken as warrant for treating that human as less valuable than others.

Objections to intrinsic dignity as a basis for action go further than pointing to its religious or quasi-religious roots. At this point, we need to return to Sulmasy's analysis. For Sulmasy, '[t]he conclusion that intrinsic dignity is the fundamental sense of dignity has significant moral implications. The notion of intrinsic dignity entails both self-regarding and other-regarding moral duties for beings that have intrinsic dignity.' Included in these are two that I want to focus on in more detail: first, the other-regarding 'obligation to respect all members of natural kinds that have intrinsic dignity', which I'll return to in a moment; and, second, the self-regarding 'duty to comport themselves in a manner that is consistent with their own intrinsic dignity'. It is this self-regarding duty that I want to focus on initially.

Self-regarding duties give rise to a significant charge of paternalism, sometimes linked to the question of how far, if at all, human dignity can be waived by an individual. Where a choice-based, autonomy approach to human rights is adopted, then it would seem strange to think that it cannot be waived by the person whose dignity is supposedly in issue. On the other hand, a more communitarian approach to dignity, or one based on Sulmasy's self-regarding duty, seems potentially compatible with an individual's not being permitted to waive his or her dignity. We are used to viewing certain rights as not at the disposal of the individual, for example the right not to be enslaved cannot be waived. In Germany, the Constitutional Court has held that 'human dignity means not only the individual dignity of the person but the dignity of man as a species. Dignity is therefore not at the disposal of the individual.' The obligation on the state to protect human dignity may justify limiting the rights of the person whom the state seeks to protect, irrespective of the preferences of the individual. The Federal Administrative Court, for example, has held that the dignity of women who work in 'peep shows' exposing themselves to men for payment is violated and they can legitimately be prohibited from doing so. A prohibition on dwarf-throwing, as part of a commercial entertainment, by a local authority in France was upheld by both the Conseil d'État and, subsequently, by the Human Rights Committee on the ground that the restriction was justified on the basis of human dignity. Such decisions have encouraged the view that the use of intrinsic dignity may produce strikingly illiberal results, contrary to human rights protections rather than examples of such protections.

This scepticism is not confined to the implications of intrinsic dignity embracing self-regarding duties. We saw earlier that dignity has been viewed as a principled basis of support for the human rights enterprise. In practice, however, dignity's *other*-regarding duties have also come to be used as a major constraint on (some) rights. Dignity sometimes functions as a justification for limiting the protection of rights or obligations, similar to a public order or public morals exception, allowing the state to place limits on what particular rights would otherwise require. In the Israeli context, human dignity has been developed not only as a basis for rights but also as a constraint on rights, leading to decisions in which pornographic films could legitimately be censored where they were regarded as degrading to human dignity, especially the dignity of women. The concept of human dignity, viewed in this way, has been seen as threatening the freedom of scientific inquiry, for example, and progress in the development of techniques that would enable a vastly increased possibility of choice for individuals in the areas of reproduction and biomedical practice. The use of dignity in restricting such research is sometimes seen as depending on a particular *anthropological* understanding of the person to ground an understanding of what human dignity requires. To put it another way, they rely on a particular understanding of what the 'natural kind' of humans involves. This has been seen by some as justifying the charge that intrinsic dignity's ontological understanding of the human is riven with unacceptable 'moralism'.

UNDERSTANDINGS OF DIGNITY IN THE SECULAR HUMAN RIGHTS CONTEXT

Intrinsic dignity is not entirely absent from human rights adjudication and interpretation. There are elements of intrinsic dignity present in some of the judicial approaches on display, most notably in the central place that Justice Aharon Barak gave to the idea in the Israeli Supreme Court's targeted killings case. Where the courts tackle the ontological question, however, they have a tendency to turn intrinsic dignity into autonomy, in the sense that the essence of what it means to be human is to be an autonomous individual. We see this approach adopted particularly in some judgments in the US Supreme Court. There, dignity has surfaced particularly in cases dealing with abortion, physician-assisted suicide, and most recently in cases dealing with gay rights, such as the recent same-sex marriage case. Justice Kennedy seems to be particularly enamoured of the concept.

That said, the more common judicial practice is not to engage with the understanding of the human as of intrinsic value. There appears to be an emerging consensus that the better approach to analysing the utility of dignity as a concept which brings added value is to focus on '*attributed* dignity' leaving 'intrinsic dignity' to one side. From this perspective, 'human dignity' involves treating people 'with respect'. The idea of respect, avoiding the exposure of others to shame and humiliation, is swiftly becoming a central understanding of the idea of human dignity in the human rights context. Prominent recent examples illustrate the idea of dignity as treating others with respect.

Jeremy Waldron, in a splendid series of lectures and articles, has argued for an understanding of dignity that is not based on the inherent moral worth of human persons, but based rather on the origins of the concept of dignity in status and rank. Human dignity, he argues, involves a requirement to accord to others the respect that would previously only have been shown to aristocrats and those of a high rank and status. Waldron is not alone in emphasizing the centrality of respect to dignity. Michael Rosen's book, which is also a major contribution to the scholarly literature on dignity, is somewhat similar. He too prefers dignity to be used to express a relatively limited understanding: that persons are entitled to be treated *with* dignity, i.e. they should be treated with proper respect, and 'most importantly, they should not be treated disrespectfully by being humiliated or degraded'. For Rosen, the wrong that is involved in not treating someone with respect is, essentially, an expressive or symbolic harm. This conception of dignity, he writes, 'emphasizes the value of the symbolic or expressive aspects of our behavior towards others'. Rosen distinguishes between this idea of dignity and regarding dignity as 'the central core of value behind human rights in general', because not all 'violations of basic rights [are] symbolic harms'. He regards dignitary harms, conceived in this way, as important in part because 'such denials of dignity may clear the psychological pathway to evil': by dehumanizing an individual or a group, it is easier to kill and torture them. Meir Dan-Cohen put it somewhat similarly some years earlier in his discussion of the role of dignity as a basis for the criminal law. He defined dignity as: 'an expressive value demanding that people's behaviour, physical and verbal, convey a certain attitude to other people, namely an attitude of respect'.

This understanding of dignity seems also to have found its way into legal and judicial discourse, as Tarun Khaitan's important article about the use of human dignity in the context of the adjudication and interpretation of human rights *law* suggests. The legal conception of dignity, he writes, 'is likely to be expressive in character', by which he means that, 'whether an act disrespects someone's dignity depends on the *meaning* that such an act expresses'. Dignity 'takes seriously', he writes, 'the expression of disrespect/insult/humiliation etc to a cherished person, object or value'. Although not all 'legal conceptions of dignity are necessarily expressive', it is the expressive conception of dignity that 'can make a distinctive contribution to human rights law. If dignity is not expressive, there is little it does that other [non-expressive] values cannot do on their own.' He continues: 'As an expressive norm, dignity brings something quite unique to the moral high table.' In the Court of Appeal in *Ladele*, Lord Neuberger MR regarded this dignity test as 'support[ing] the view that Ms Ladele's proper and genuine desire to have her religious views relating to marriage respected should not be permitted to override Islington's concern to ensure that all its registrars manifest equal respect for the homosexual community as for the heterosexual community'.

OBJECTIONS TO DIGNITY AS RESPECT

There is, however, a consistent drumbeat of concern that this conception of dignity, understood in the sense of the attribution of dignity to others, and the resulting 'respect' that is due, also has the capacity to be highly illiberal. Whether a particular act conveys disrespect, sufficient to amount to a wrong against dignity, at least as interpreted from a strong expressivist perspective, requires a determination as to the social and cultural meaning of the action taken. This in turn requires a choice to be made as to what is the relevant community of interpretation, within which the question of social meaning is to be determined. There are various different ways in which this might be determined. It might involve considering the social meaning within the society as a whole. But that gives rise to the concern that dignity simply dissolves into moral populism.

To avoid this challenge, strong expressionism may privilege the social meaning of an action *as understood by particular subcommunities*. The social meaning of an objection to same-sex marriage might be assessed, for example, from the perspective of gay groups. But that is also not without considerable difficulties. There is, to begin with, an important question as to *which* groups' social understanding should be prioritized. The plethora of different subcommunities, each of which may attribute a different 'meaning' to the action, may itself encourage particular subcommunities to become ever more assertive of their understanding of the social meaning that they attribute to the action, to ensure that their understanding is not drowned out by the contrasting understandings of other subgroups. For Khaitan, in emphasizing 'offensiveness' a strong expressivist interpretation of dignity may encourage what he terms 'respect inflation', by which he means that there is a danger of 'encouraging a culture where people are easily offended' and where they seek to use the law to prevent such offence.

The strong expressivist dignity principle may have another effect. Lauded as a basis for expanding the reach of human rights, or at least for stabilizing its existing scope, dignity as respect risks being turned into a mechanism that *reduces* its scope, particularly if it limits autonomy or welfare. Khaitan identifies a 'liberal worry' that a strong expressivist approach to dignity has 'serious implications for a person's freedom of expression'. And also, we might add, for their expression of religious sensibilities (think of Ms Ladele). If the lack of respect communicated to the 'victim' subcommunity becomes the core of dignity, but dignity is still seen as the core of human rights, then we may also end up concentrating only on expressively conceived dignitary harms and neglecting the rest. Being required to twist everything else in human rights law into a 'respect' perspective would be enormously limiting and ultimately unconvincing.

More importantly, perhaps, the recognition that there are strongly competing understandings of social meaning may precipitate a slide into relativism, or at least into such a high degree of context specificity that dignity's claim to universalism would be severely tested, if not destroyed. Khaitan denies that expressivism is relativistic, in that the 'meanings of actions have to be determined objectively'. Rosen, too, accepts that 'what expresses contempt for human beings varies . . . between cultures and contexts' but that does not mean it is relativistic. I agree that strong expressivism is not moral relativism in the sense that different moral norms apply to different societies. But strong expressivism does involve a norm that *in practice* may give wildly different solutions to similar problems in different contexts. Although the strong expressivist dignity test applied may be of universal significance, the message the action communicates 'derives from the cultural setting in which it is performed'. *That* meaning is likely to vary considerably from country to country, leading to radically different results from the application of the dignity principle to otherwise similar situations. Not moral relativism in theory perhaps but, apparently, highly relativistic in practice.

PLACE OF RELIGION IN WHAT IT MEANS TO BE HUMAN

Finally, there is a dimension of the ontological difficulty which haunts all of the religious litigation that we have encountered so far. If we say that an intrinsic understanding of human dignity underpins human rights, or even that dignity as respect, is a core value, the question arises: what attitude should we take to claims of religious conscience and the like? Is religion central to our view of what it means to be human, and are protections for religion central, therefore, to the human rights enterprise? Is a core implication of what it means to treat someone with respect that we allow them to practise their religion unimpeded? Or should we, rather, view religion as marginal, or even contrary to our conception of what it means to be fully human, and query whether religion should be the beneficiary of human rights protections at all?

References to the centrality of religion to our understanding of what it means to be human are not entirely absent from human rights adjudication and interpretation. The approach taken by Sachs J in the South African Constitutional Court decision in *Christian Education South Africa* v. *Minister of Education* has elements of this understanding. 'The right to believe or not to believe', he said:

> and to act or not to act according to his or her beliefs or non-beliefs, is one of the key ingredients of any person's dignity. Yet freedom of religion goes beyond protecting the inviolability of the individual conscience. For many believers, their relationship with God or creation is central to all their activities. It concerns their capacity to relate in an intensely meaningful fashion to their sense of themselves, their community and their universe. For millions in all walks of life, religion provides support and nurture and a framework for individual and social stability and growth. Religious belief has the capacity to awake concepts

of self-worth and human dignity which form the cornerstone of human rights. It affects the believer's view of society and founds the distinction between right and wrong. It expresses itself in the affirmation and continuity of powerful traditions that frequently have an ancient character transcending historical epochs and national boundaries.

That said, there is a clearly differing position emerging between human rights law and, for example, the Catholic Church in how religion is to be considered. From the Church's perspective, two different elements appear to be crucial. First, religious freedom is seen as a foundational right because it is a fundamental expression of a person's *nature*—the unrestricted search for God and truth. If this right is not recognized, if that search is unjustifiably impeded, then a person's capacity to realize his or her own nature (to strive towards perfection) is thwarted. Leaving aside the reference to 'human nature', always problematic in a legal context, this is otherwise just about compatible with the secular autonomy argument, but there is a more second problematic issue. In Catholic doctrine, autonomy and freedom cannot be the sole basis for religious freedom, because commitment to freedom needs to be tempered by the knowledge that freedom can be subverted and instrumentalized if it is not seen in its correct relationship with *truth*.

Secular human rights judges, on the other hand, would be unlikely to regard religious liberty as the 'source and synthesis' of other personal rights, as *Centesimus Annus*, one of the key documents in Catholic doctrine, does. The understanding of what 'religion' is also appears to differ significantly in the two traditions, with the legal view, as we saw in the previous chapter, sometimes viewing religion in highly individualistic terms, classifying religion together with many other forms of chosen 'beliefs'. There is a major divide, too, as to why religion should be defended in a human rights context. Human rights law sees 'religion and belief' as legitimately protected, but often only as expressions of autonomy.

PROPORTIONALITY

The argument advanced in the previous paragraphs is stated at a relatively high level of generality, but this is not just a theoretical problem. The courts dealing with religious litigation are faced with this problem in just about every piece of religious litigation we have considered. This is because of the central role that the concept of proportionality plays in such litigation.

We saw in Chapter 4 how the ECHR contains several different kinds of rights. We distinguished between 'absolute' rights, such as the right to be free from torture, in the sense that the right has such weight that no other consideration is sufficiently important for it to trump that right, from 'qualified' rights. We saw that the right to freedom of religion in the ECHR is primarily of the second type, as is the right to be free from religious discrimination. Qualified rights also include rights such as the right to a private life, the right to freedom of speech, and the right to freedom of assembly. Qualified rights are structured so that other considerations can be taken into account in determining whether that right has been breached. The way in which limitations on such rights is drafted (any limitations on the right must be 'necessary in a democratic society') leads the European Court of Human Rights to test for 'proportionality': that is, the Court considers whether the purpose of the limitation of the right is legitimate, whether the limitation is necessary for attaining that purpose, and whether the measure strikes a proper balance between that purpose and the right that is being restricted. 'Qualified' rights, we saw, are thus highly contextualized, requiring judgements to be made about how the right is to be exercised in particular situations, and the limits on that right.

The approach a court takes to the ontological question significantly affects the way in which the court addresses the proportionality exercise. The more importance the court places on religion, the more weight it has; the more weight it has, the more those limiting religious practices and beliefs must show that that limitation is justified, despite the effect of those limitations on those practices and beliefs. The courts seldom address this weighting in any methodical or systematic way, but the relative weights are pretty clearly identifiable in practice, given the result of the proportionality analysis. We have seen earlier that the British Court cannot have accorded any significant weight to the religious community's view that the cow that was to be killed was sacred, given the relative ease with which the court found that the protection of the local economy from the ravages of disease weighed more heavily than the survival of the sacred cow.

Another example further illustrates the point. In the *Ashers* case, the owners of a cake shop were found to have discriminated unlawfully on the grounds of sexual orientation. They argued that, even if there was unlawful discrimination, their freedom of religion protected them. They set out their religious beliefs, which included a belief that marriage should only be between a man and a woman. As part of their faith they believed it would be sinful for them to say or do anything which had the intention or effect of promoting gay sexual relations or same-sex marriage, and that included printing a slogan supporting same sex-marriage on a cake. The Court of Appeal disagreed. The Court identified the issue as where to strike a balance between the prohibition of discrimination on the grounds of sexual orientation in the provision of goods, facilities, and service, and the protection of religion, belief, and conscience. The Court held that the principal issue in this context is whether there is a reasonable relationship of proportionality between the means employed and the aim sought to be achieved. It concluded that there was, considering the bakers' objection to providing a message with which they disagreed because of their deeply held religious beliefs as clearly outweighed, among other things, by the need to eradicate arbitrary discrimination in the commercial sphere. A different weighting of the claims of religious conscience, and its centrality to human dignity would equally clearly have resulted in a different result.

PART III

WAYS FORWARD

7

FUNDAMENTALS OF HUMAN RIGHTS THEORY

The assumption, common some years ago, that Western liberal democracies had solved the problem of the relationship between state and religion, with constitutional secularism as a main plank of the solution, now seems somewhat naïve and precipitous, akin to confident declarations of the 'end of history'. Similarly, the days when the relationship between *human rights law* and religion was a quiet backwater, appearing to confirm arguments about the end of religion as a serious force in the world, are long gone, and 'religious litigation' is on the rise.

I hope I have persuaded you, on the basis of what I have said so far, that the relationship between human rights and religion in the judicial context is complex, changing, and problematic. My basic argument so far has been that the relationship between human rights and religion is becoming more conflictual for reasons having to do with the changing role of religion, and the changing role of human rights. The courts are intimately involved in adjudicating these conflicts, and in some cases they are centre stage, due to the changing institutional opportunity structure for litigation, both national and transnational. Although there is an overlapping human rights consensus between the main religions and human rights institutions, the current pattern of the relationship between human rights and religion is changing, and the hard-fought cases we have discussed are not simply anomalies.

In the previous three chapters, I have described three particular and, I argued, *central* problems that recur when courts have to deal with religious litigation: the teleological problem, the epistemological problem, and the ontological problem. All three problems are both the occasion for disputes, and (taken together) exacerbate other disputes, bringing the courts themselves into the fray,

Litigating Religions: An Essay on Human Rights, Courts, and Beliefs. Christopher McCrudden. © Christopher McCrudden 2018. Published 2018 by Oxford University Press.

preventing them from playing the role of standing above the conflict. So, what is to be done?

The temptation at this point is to introduce some *deus ex machina*, some device whereby an apparently insoluble conflict is unexpectedly solved by the contrived introduction of some new idea. The suggestions I'm about to make are not of this type, in two respects. We have already identified many of these methods previously; none should come as a surprise. As importantly, these suggestions will not 'solve' the problem, but rather only provide mechanisms by which the tensions I've identified may be addressed in a way that may prove more productive than the approaches adopted up to now have proved to be. So, what am I suggesting?

RETHINKING THE FOUNDATIONS

It is time to set the issues I've raised within the broader human rights debate. I suggest that the tense relationship between religion and human rights has resulted, at least in part, because the conflicts engendered relate to fundamental (and, so far, unresolved) issues that go to the heart of the human rights project itself. In the previous chapter, I suggested that the issue of what it means to be human has been a critically important area of dispute between secular and religious conceptions of human rights. Although there appears to be a common approach to the issue, in that both religious and secular understandings of human rights often resort to the concept of human dignity as a way of addressing that issue, human dignity has contributed little to the development of a consensus on the problem, and no common conception of dignity is yet discernible. Dignity discourse has, so far at least, done little to provide a conception with significant enough substantive content to solve the most profound issues in the judicial resolution of human rights claims: the appropriate balance between the individual and the community, including such questions as the appropriate limits on individual freedom; the appropriateness of the use of state power to ensure basic standards of material security; what rights should be attributed at the beginning of life and at the end of life; and how far we have responsibilities to ourselves and to others. On these, and other important human rights issues, disputes will continue, in part because of the absence of a common approach to the ontological question.

We must, therefore, revisit the ontological problem if we are to make progress, but my approach will be initially indirect, and I will approach the problem by thinking more about the nature of human rights.

Human rights, it is clear, are a subset of rights in general, but what type of rights are 'human' rights, as opposed to other sorts of rights, such as the rights of citizens, or the rights of corporations, or the rights of states? Some of the implications of focusing on the 'human' in human rights are fairly obvious. If a particular subset of rights applies only to humans, that means that they don't apply to non-humans, but what types of creatures are not 'human'? Animals, presumably, but all animals? Foetuses? Those in a permanent vegetative state? These are some of the most controversial political questions, particularly in the culture wars, and they are deeply contested. But the issue of the human in human rights gets even more difficult when we remember that at least since the Universal Declaration of Human Rights in 1948, human rights are said to be founded on the principle of 'human dignity'. Again, that word, 'human'. So, the concept of the 'human' is built into the deep foundations of the idea of human rights, as well as the practice of human rights on a day-to-day basis.

The problem that we identified in the previous chapter is, in part, that as the power of the human rights ideal has grown, as human rights have come to occupy more and more space in political and legal debate, the concept of the 'human' seems to be less clear, rather than more clear. What we have, in practice, is a significantly fractured set of responses to what the 'human' in human rights and in human dignity supposes. In most jurisdictions, animals do not fall within the protection of human rights and human dignity, but not in all. In some jurisdictions, foetuses are protected by the right to life, but comparatively few. Those in a permanent vegetative state may or may not be regarded as having the same human rights as those not in that condition. And so on.

With the expansion of human rights, the more contested it has become, and the more we need a good explanation of why human rights are normatively justified, if they are. Human rights are now more contested than ever, not least in the United Kingdom, and the absence of a good normative explanation risks undermining the project. If we can't come up with a good explanation as to why human rights are a good thing, then what right do we have to force them on others, whether in Syria or in Belfast? And in attempting to provide such an explanation we almost immediately confront the question of the 'human'.

Let's step back from the most controversial questions for a moment and begin with the basics. Human rights should not be seen as exclusively or purely the creation of law. Nor should rights be subject to the whim of shifting majorities. Whatever the benefits of democracy, majoritarian preferences should not be seen alone as the basis for human rights standards. Democracy has important limits, and one of those limits is in the area of human rights. So, if human rights are based neither exclusively in law, nor determined by the principle of majority rule, on what exactly are they based? We have examined previously what might be called the 'orthodox' answer to this question, which is to suggest that human rights are those rights that attach to humans simply on the basis of their humanity, and for no other reason. This is sometimes also termed the 'naturalistic' justification, because it is based on an understanding of human nature. There are, of course, many naturalistic or orthodox theories. We saw that one variant of this is that human rights are derived from the idea of 'human dignity'. We saw that naturalistic approaches may be either metaphysical or non-metaphysical. Some argue that the concept of dignity depends on a metaphysical understanding of the human in relation to a deity. But there are also non-metaphysical understandings of 'human dignity' that are nevertheless naturalistic, where the dignity of the person is seen to derive from an understanding of what it means to be human, based on our observations of human experience.

But there are now sustained attempts by political philosophers to theorize about the meaning, scope, and justification of human rights on an *alternative* basis. One significant difference between these different philosophical approaches has to do with methodology: where do we start if we want to provide a normative account of human rights? Philosophers who adopt the orthodox, naturalistic account often base their account initially on a priori reasoning (what I'll call practice-*in*dependent theories). But a more recent strand of philosophical theorizing has attempted to provide accounts that begin from the *practice* of human rights (practice-*dependent* theories), where what human rights are, and how they are to be justified are to be considered from the bottom-up: we should derive our normative justification from the practice of human rights, rather than using our normative justification to limit what should correctly be termed human rights. A prominent example of a practice-dependent theory is that of Charles Beitz, following John Rawls, where human rights are seen in practice as identifying those norms that would justify international intervention in another state to protect the state's own population against abuses.

There are significant shortcomings in practice-dependent philosophical accounts up to now. First, recent philosophical accounts of human rights that purport to be based on the actual practice of human rights are flawed, in so far as they seldom engage in a sustained way with the national and international *judicial* interpretation of human rights guarantees, focusing instead mainly on the international political practice of human rights, or on the text of human rights treaties, or on the limited judicial practice of one state, or on historical developments without appreciating the role of judicial practice in that history. Second, current practice-dependent philosophical approaches give too little weight to actual legal practice, since, were they to do so, they would not be quite as dismissive of 'orthodox', or practice-independent, approaches as they are. In other words, current practice-dependent approaches are incomplete as they stand at the moment. Third, a broader understanding of what constitutes relevant practice (including judicial practice, for example) would also require practice-dependent theories to confront the significant degree of substantive pluralism in our understandings of human rights as currently interpreted. Fourth, a broader understanding of that practice would also take more seriously still the institutional context in which human rights operate. For example, philosophical approaches require a deeper engagement with the fact that judicial institutions are so heavily involved. This poses a challenge in particular to those seeking to reconcile human rights with ideas of democratic participation. How exactly, for example, does judicial independence cohere with a deep commitment to the democratic method?

There is a fifth problem, however, that is of particular relevance to the scope of this essay. With some notable exceptions (Hans Joas, Charles Taylor, John Milbank, Nicholas Wolterstorff come to mind), human rights theorizing based on human rights practice often regards the *religious* practice of human rights as embarrassing at best, malign at worst. The philosophical case for excluding religious understandings of human rights was put by John Rawls. When we were considering the epistemological problem, we identified an approach which involved the courts redefining religious arguments to conform to an idea of 'public reasons'. This idea crops up again in this context. Rawls argued that citizens engaged in certain political activities have a duty of civility which requires that they be able to justify their decisions on fundamental political issues by reference *only* to *public* values and *public* standards. This would exclude, in fact was possibly intended to exclude, religious narratives of human rights.

So far, then, I have suggested that recent philosophical accounts of human rights that purport to be based on the 'practice' of human rights (so-called 'practice-dependent' theories of human rights) are flawed, in so far as they seldom engage in a sustained way with the actual practice of human rights, and that this practice includes both national and international, legal as well as political, religious, and secular understandings. The main conclusion is that 'practice-dependent' philosophers of human rights do not practice what they preach and adopt a considerably more skewed and narrow understanding of the 'practice' of human rights than is justified, given the diversity of human rights typologies. Human rights practice has, in the main, run ahead of human rights theory.

In light of this, those purporting to ground their normative understanding of human rights in human rights practice have a clear choice: *either* they can reconsider how far they are *really* committed to basing their theories on this practice, leading them to decide ultimately to drop this structural feature of their argument. Alternatively, they may recommit to basing their understanding of human rights initially on the *actual* practice of human rights and significantly adapt their theories as a result.

My preference is for the second of these alternatives. A broader understanding of that practice would challenge some of the normative conclusions that existing practice-dependent theorists reach, as we shall see. Not engaging with the practice is too theoretically limiting.

RECONSTRUCTING A PRACTICE-DEPENDENT THEORY

What would a reconstructed practice-dependent theory of human rights look like, and how would it address issues of religion? My starting point for an attempted reconstruction distinguishes two different justificatory issues in constructing a normative theory of human rights. First, what is the 'general justifying aim' of the system? What justifies the creation and maintenance of such a system—what good can it achieve, what duty can it fulfil, what moral demand can it satisfy? Second, we need to distinguish the methods we adopt to further this system, including who may properly be accorded human rights, and how particular human rights should be determined and interpreted. We need to distinguish, in other words, the general justifying aim of the system, from how we pursue that aim. (Incidentally, Allen Buchanan's new book adopts a similar starting point, although he and I end up in significantly different places.)

My suggestion is that the general justifying aim of the practice of human rights is, indeed, the pursuit of human dignity, in the sense that each human person, *qua* human person, possesses an intrinsic worth that should be respected. Let's recollect what I suggested in the previous chapter regarding this claim. This is not an institutionalist claim, in the sense that the worth of a human person does not depend on any institutional recognition, and in that sense it is a foundationalist claim, but it is a weak foundationalist claim. In particular, we should not infer that the idea of human dignity instantiates any particular understanding of what human dignity consists in. It is not necessarily an understanding of dignity as autonomy, or of equality, or of communitarianism. In particular, it is not necessarily a *liberal* agenda. It is simply a claim that a human person has a moral worth as a person.

Recollect also that I suggested that two elements deriving from the claim to human dignity have developed which further this aim but also limit the methods of pursuing it, and these also are weak claims. First, some forms of conduct between persons are inconsistent with respect for this intrinsic worth (*the relational claim*), and, second, the state exists for the individual not *vice versa (the limited state claim)*. The fault lines lie in disagreement as to what the intrinsic worth of persons consists in, what forms of treatment are inconsistent with that worth, and what the implications are for the role of the state. The different understandings of each of these elements of the concept of human dignity indicate that different conceptions of human dignity and different ways of pursuing it are identifiable.

Weak though it is, however, the general justifying aim I've identified, human dignity, does provide a normative foundation for the system of human *rights* as a whole. Note that I distinguish between human *dignity* and human *rights*. Human rights are best thought of as concerning the delivery of the general justifying aim of protecting human dignity; human rights are to be seen as one strategy by which human dignity is pursued. Human rights are not the only way in which dignity is pursued. The human rights system consists of a set of norms that are institutionalized in related but different sets of practices: international, diplomatic, legal, constitutional, moral, revolutionary, *and religious*. In this, my approach is clearly influenced by Rawls, in the sense that human rights don't just exist out there floating free; they have to be institutionalized to make them 'real'. Where I differ from Rawls is that I do not limit the institutionalization of human rights to the narrow range of institutional practices that he does. In particular, I include religious understandings of human rights as appropriately regarded as contributing to the construction of a practice-dependent theory.

Given the pluralism of different subsystems of human rights, different rights aiming to further human dignity may (perhaps even *should*) result. Dignity may also provide a critique of the human rights system. It is perfectly compatible with my approach, indeed my approach requires, that each human rights subsystem can and should be assessed for ways in which it does *not* adequately pursue human dignity, or might better pursue human dignity. It provides, therefore, a constraint on what human rights can consist of in each of these subsystems. It would reject, for example, an attempted justification of an approach to the pursuit of human rights that simply handed all power over to an unconstrained state. But, again, this is a relatively weak constraint.

In practice, these critiques are both internal to the subsystems I have described, and external to those subsystems. Each subsystem develops over time particular ways of understanding the implications of the general justifying aim of human rights and therefore provides the opportunity for an immanent critique of the understanding of human rights within that system. But the fact that there are different subsystems means that there is the possibility that one subsystem's understanding of the general justifying aim may conflict with that of another, and this both encourages and facilitates external critique of the approach to human rights adopted in these other subsystems. The human rights system, in practice, is strongly pluralistic, not just institutionally but also normatively.

INTEGRATING 'ORTHODOX' APPROACHES

There are several particularly important respects in which this suggested revised approach has advantages, but I'll focus on only one. It helps us to go beyond the current divide between 'orthodox' and practice-dependent approaches. The sharp distinction between practice-dependent and practice-independent approaches collapses once we get to grips with the actual practice of human rights. As Liao and Etinson suggest, the contrast between political and naturalistic conceptions of human rights is 'at least overdrawn if not wholly misleading'. 'Practice-dependent' theory should be refined by the inclusion of distinctively 'orthodox' elements.

Lea Ypi has sought to present a convincing theoretical framework that would integrate both practice-dependent and practice-independent approaches, one in which space is made 'for a more dynamic reading of the relationship between political ideas and political practice'. She focuses on 'contestation' in seeking to interpret the function and purpose of institutional practices. We need to reflect critically, she argues, on *particular* conflicts. We should explore 'the different concepts protagonists invoke to render it meaningful, the kinds of theories that they deploy to explain its occurrence, and ... the interpretive paradigms upon which a combination of all these features eventually relies'. Examining these contestations is critical because it enables us to identify how 'the relation between preservation and innovation of principles unfolds given particular practices: it helps to clarify, for example, which conceptual categories of the past are eliminated or shown to be morally problematic, and which ones are emphasized, updated, or invented from scratch'.

She insists, rightly in my view, that 'one needs to give more careful thought to the way the ideal and non-ideal approaches reciprocally interact'. For Ypi, ideal and non-ideal roughly correspond with practice independent and practice dependent respectively. In the conflicts that we analyse, she suggests, we will see how various interpretations of the function and purpose of current institutions will be advanced.

> If these interpretations are inadequate or unable to capture emerging claims and concerns, the groups who are most affected by the conflict will contest the meaning or conceptual categories associated with them. They will ... attempt to appropriate these categories and to interpret them in a different way—a way that tries to link them to first-order ideal principles and seeks to promote an alternative set of claims.

This will all seem quite technical philosophy, but the point is important. Putting it somewhat simplistically, what she is suggesting is that institutions change and move on in part by incorporating externally generated normative standards. The implication is that, in the legal context, and I suspect in at least some religious contexts, changes in human rights interpretation occur in part when these bodies incorporate elements of orthodox human rights thinking into their practice. A practice-based approach to human rights must, therefore, recognize that human rights practice is itself sensitive to naturalistic orthodoxy, and that the supposed sharp dichotomy between practice-dependent and practice-independent approaches is therefore exaggerated.

INTEGRATING PLURALISM

My suggested approach accepts that human rights law and human rights practice beyond the legal sphere is, indeed, pluralistic, and argues that this pluralism is not randomly chaotic, or dysfunctional, or temporary. Building this pluralism into human rights theory thus accurately reflects the diverse nature of human rights, including judicial adjudication and religious narratives within that system. From this perspective, human rights is seen as providing a forum in which tensions and conflicts over some of the most basic epistemological and ontological questions are engaged. From this perspective, it would be puzzling if a highly pluralistic system of human rights (or perhaps it would be better to describe it as a set of associated communities of human rights) had *not* emerged. The pluralism of the system is not, therefore, a problem to be overcome, but a critically important and central aspect not only of the proper understanding of human rights law but also of human rights as a whole, one to be recognized and cherished for the critical reflexive function it encourages.

My preferred approach is dialogic. This should not be confused with a *dialectic* process, despite the fact that both critically emphasize the importance of conflict and tension. The goal of a dialectic process is to arrive, via conflict and tension, at a *solution* to the apparent conflict, a solution that establishes primacy over other solutions. In a dialogic process, on the other hand, various 'solutions' coexist in tension with each other, and continue to do so. One solution may hold more salience than another in particular circumstances, but it may be supplanted if the preferred strategy does not have the desired effect of providing a forum in which those in conflict continue to engage. For Richard Sennett, the dialectic approach attempts to lead to closure and resolution, whereas in a dialogic process differences can remain essentially unresolved at a fundamental level. But, under my preferred approach, the lack of resolution of the contradictions in human rights disputes is not to be regarded as a failure, but rather as essential to the system. The practice of human rights adjudication, human rights law, and human rights courts become the site of a provisional and (politically) temporary accommodation that helps us to live together, despite the basic conflicts that are brought to court; we agree to abide by the decisions of a decision maker whom we agree, for the moment at least, is broadly legitimate and competent. Human rights adjudication is seen as an enterprise in which the judge is not only engaging with the dispute in hand, attempting to arrive at a justified and reasoned judgment, but doing so in a context in which the nature of the judge's resolution of the question is (politically) provisional.

My preferred approach is not, therefore, a static model, but one open to continuing change, including change involving the continued suitability of human rights law itself to provide the forum in which these contested questions are considered at all. Not only is the actual result in a particular case open to revision, but the judge's legitimacy in arriving at the decision at all is also provisional. That is an important and defensible role for human rights law, and human rights courts, but it is a modest one.

The danger with this approach is that it may appear to legitimize a highly relativistic critique of human rights law, in which the failures of human rights law are construed as a necessary part of the system, therefore delegitimizing the enterprise. I do not think this is so, not least because the emphasis on the temporary and provisional nature of human rights law, and therefore the possibility of an external critique of any particular human rights subsystem, including human rights law, offers hope for the disappointed and a spur to activists to change the interpretation, and even the system, and argue for a better resolution. Perhaps most importantly, my preferred approach leaves open a view of human rights as political and moral and legal and social *and religious*, one in which debate is encouraged within and between these arenas of discourse, as to what human dignity requires.

Dignity, therefore, has the added function of challenging and disrupting apparently settled positions. Dignity has the capacity and role of serving as the basis for critique of societally determined understandings of human rights, whether they are religious, or legal, or political. Dignity may also, therefore, cut across rights, keeping human rights concepts from becoming unquestioned. Dignity may, indeed, outstrip rights. It may, then, function in some way as a ground for rights but also a ground for the critique of rights. Thus, for example, those who consider that dignity protects the integrity of the human person will be able to use the concept of dignity to criticize an interpretation of rights that is too cramped to protect that person, or to criticize a claimed extension of rights that seems not to reflect or protect human dignity. So, dignity will help to provide a certain kind of critical distance from rights, reducing the tendency to fetishize rights in contemporary society. This does not, however, necessarily undermine the argument that dignity is a foundation for rights. If dignity is part of the foundation, it can provide a basis for criticism of current interpretations of specific rights.

8

HOW SHOULD COURTS APPROACH RELIGIOUS LITIGATION?

One important implication that arises from the previous chapter is that the institutional context is vital for understanding the normative pluralism of human rights practice. The pursuit of human dignity through advancing human rights is not only constrained by the normative understandings of each institution and its institutional logic, but also by the degree to which these institutions are open to normative influence from other institutions. In practice, human rights arise out of contestation, power struggles, and ideological conflict within *and between* institutions. And some (indeed, many) of those conflicts concern the very understanding of what it means to respect the worth of the human person. Discourse, debate, and contestation are not marginal to the practice of human rights, but central to it, and this contestation takes place as much between as within particular institutional subsystems.

The previous chapter had relatively little to say about the role of *courts* in this system, except that courts should be recognized explicitly as contributors to human rights discourse. Nothing was said, however, about whether courts are a better forum for human rights discourse than other forums such as the legislature, or civil society more broadly. So, nothing in the previous chapter determines whether religious litigation should be a *preferred* forum for addressing actual conflicts between religious beliefs and practice and human rights norms. My own view is that in many cases courts are indeed a comparatively poor forum in which to engage in these debates, and I would sometimes prefer that the necessary compromises would be worked out in other forums, such as democratic legislatures. My judgement, however, is that, for many of the reasons discussed in Chapter 3, courts will in practice

Litigating Religions: An Essay on Human Rights, Courts, and Beliefs. Christopher McCrudden. © Christopher McCrudden 2018. Published 2018 by Oxford University Press.

continue to be centrally involved in such debates, for good or ill. We should recognize that this is likely and attempt to create the circumstances in which judicial involvement in such disputes is less problematic than we have seen it is at present.

In this chapter and the next, I suggest that the theory of human rights proposed in the previous chapter has important implications for those who are involved in religious litigation, those on the religious side of the debates, those on the human rights side of the debates, and for the courts which need to adjudicate such disputes. In this chapter, I focus on the implications the theory has for courts, and in particular what role religious understandings of human rights and human dignity should play in this process.

ROLE OF RELIGIOUS NARRATIVES IN HUMAN RIGHTS DISCOURSE

We saw earlier that the European Court of Human Rights (ECtHR) considers that freedom of religion is important not only because it furthers the freedom of individuals, but also because it is in the interests of society as a whole. While the Court said that 'religious freedom is primarily a matter of individual conscience' it went on to say that the value of the collective aspect of freedom of religion goes beyond safeguarding the particular individual or the particular religious community in question. We have seen that the Court considered that 'it is also a precious asset for atheists, agnostics, sceptics, and the unconcerned. The *pluralism* indissociable from a democratic society, which has been dearly won over the centuries, depends on it.' 'Indeed', the Court continues, 'the autonomous existence of religious communities is indispensable for pluralism in a democratic society'. We might add, following the logic of the previous chapter, that it is also indispensable for developing an understanding of human rights and human dignity.

The importance of religion, from this perspective, is not only because of its role in forming the identity or self-perception of human beings, and not only to protect the autonomy of religious institutions, but because it is important for human beings to make sense of their life in a more comprehensive sense. To do so necessarily transcends the domain of what we know, perhaps even of what we *can* know. The opportunity to develop views about our place in life and the universe and to contest those views, is important for self-understanding. It is essential that there is room for debate in the public space about our outlooks on the world. And if the opportunity for self-understanding is the justification, religion must be available because that is one of the forums in which such concerns are explored. The importance of religious freedom for those who are not religious is the possibility it offers to engage with alternative views on the world and our place in it. An openness to different world-views is a condition for self-understanding.

With some notable exceptions, the theoretical literature emanating from the human rights side of the debate has, however, been distorted by a lack of sympathy for the potential importance for non-believers of religious thought. This lack of sympathy has contributed to a sustained attempt to keep human rights 'pure', free from serious consideration of how religious thought might contribute an alternative perspective on issues of current concern. This is why, in part, we have the lack of theoretical progress I identified earlier, and muddled our thinking on both human rights and religion. The aim, instead, should be to identify strategies that enable a genuine dialogue to take place over precisely that most contested of all questions in human rights, what it means to be human. This has implications for how dialogue is conceptualized and practised, by organized religion, the courts, and the academic community. By imaginative sympathy by the legal with the religious internal point of view (and by the religious with the legal internal view, to be considered in the next chapter), we should be able to make theoretical progress.

IS DIALOGUE POSSIBLE?

A central question is whether, in the debates between religion and the reconceptualized human rights I suggest, a true dialogue is possible, and what would be necessary to secure such a dialogue. Bradford Hinze contrasts two approaches to communication: 'a dialogic mode ... in which messages oscillate between participants, and discursive modes, in which a message flows from sender to receiver'. In the latter, '[s]peakers are not required to listen and listeners are not required to speak. There is no open-ended mutuality, no chance for all parties to learn, for participants to be influenced by each other leading to mutual growth.' Hinze crucially distinguishes between two different ways in which 'dialogue' has come to be understood. One mode of dialogue 'draws on classical Platonic, Augustinian, and personalist theories of dialogue', and is seen as 'able to guarantee and safeguard the weight of *truth* in dialogue'. Another mode of dialogue is seen 'risk[ing] placing the truth of tradition in jeopardy'. The former, according to Hinze, is a 'medium for transmitting and conveying the truth of tradition already established', as opposed to the latter that advances 'an approach to dialogue [that is] interested not only in handing on but also in generating, developing, or revising the truth of the living tradition'. Hinze does not regard the former as constituting 'true' dialogue, and I am equally sceptical.

In the next chapter, we shall consider the problems in engaging religions in true dialogue (which are substantial, I admit). The problem in engaging in a true dialogue is not confined to religious actors, however. We find a degree of fundamentalism on both the religious and the human rights sides of the discourse. When both sides claim to speak the truth, but 'the truths' appear to conflict, the stage is set for a stand-off, which may prove difficult to resolve. There is an unfortunate human rights tradition that sees human rights as advancing a 'comprehensive ideology', as Michael McConnell has called it, in which there are 'right answers' to be found. This approach is the basis for what some have called the new civil religion of 'human rights'. Giorgio Sacerdoti has described how, in his view, '[t]he "religion" of human rights and fundamental freedoms has replaced other religions and beliefs as the underpinning of social life in contemporary societies'. This approach must be overcome if progress is to be made.

How should human rights be *practised*, if we are to take seriously the idea of a true dialogue between secular and religious understandings of human rights? In particular, to quote Michael Ignatieff again, how can we best 'stop thinking of human rights as trumps and begin thinking of them as a language that creates the basis for deliberation'? If we aim to engage in a genuine dialogue in human rights practice, what are the practical implications for the courts' role? I suggest that taking three concepts more seriously would be an important starting point: pluralism, secularity, and accommodation.

PLURALISM REVISITED

We have seen earlier that the ECtHR has viewed the collective aspect of freedom of religion as going beyond safeguarding the particular religious community in question, considering that 'The pluralism indissociable from a democratic society, which has been dearly won over the centuries, depends on it.' For the ECtHR, this 'pluralism', we saw, is built 'on the genuine recognition of, and respect for, diversity and the dynamics of cultural traditions, ethnic and cultural identities, religious beliefs, artistic, literary and socio-economic ideas and concepts'. Although adopted in the context of freedom of religion, this approach also seems particularly well suited to becoming the appropriate *telos* of Article 14's prohibition of religious discrimination, and it would not require too significant a shift of perspective. In particular, the idea of 'diversity' is one that has already found a home in the anti-discrimination context. Taken seriously, viewing the *telos* of religious anti-discrimination law as one of protecting 'pluralism' in this sense, could have significant effects in reorienting the interpretation of religious anti-discrimination law. Without attempting to be complete, there are several particular elements of a revised approach that should follow if pluralism were to become the *telos* of both freedom of religion and non-discrimination on the basis of religion.

SECULARITY

There is a critical distinction between two different conceptions of what a secular state should aspire to look like. One possibility is what we might call 'secularity', and the other is a more comprehensive substantive viewpoint, which we can term 'secularism'. Brett Scharffs has explained this distinction in detail elsewhere, but (in summary) 'secularism' refers to an ideological position that is committed to promoting a secular order. Secularism is itself a positive ideology. The state is committed to opposing religiously based or religiously motivated reasoning by political actors, hostility to religion in public life, an insistence that religious manifestation should be relegated to an ever-shrinking sphere of private life, and sometimes to an aggressive proselytizing atheism—what has been called 'secular fundamentalism'.

By contrast, 'secularity' means an approach to religion–state relations that avoids identification of the state with any particular religion or ideology (including secularism itself) and endeavours to provide a framework capable of accommodating a broad range of religions and ideological beliefs. Secularity is a more modest concept, committed to creating what might be called a broad realm of 'constitutional and legal space' in which competing conceptions of the good (some religious, some not) may be worked out in theory and lived in practice by their proponents, adherents, and critics. Those committed to secularity consider it to be preferable to secularism as a guide to the right relationship between religion and the state because we should be sceptical of state-adopted utopian visions, and distrust those who seek to compel the state implementation of an all-embracing vision of the good or right.

The first element in a revised approach involves replacing 'secularism' with 'secularity' as the appropriate aim for the relationship between state authority and religion in the public sphere. Secularism, in other words, should not become the state religion—explicitly or implicitly. The state should not attempt to promote a pristine secular order where the public realm is scrubbed clean of all religious residue. This is not only a dystopian vision of neutrality, which is often defined in terms of what is excluded rather than by what is included, it is not really 'neutrality' at all, at least in any satisfying sense of the term. The reason secularity is a more attractive ideal is because it is *not* an ideology, but rather a framework for pluralism. If it is a conception of the good, it is a thin one. It does not say there is no 'truth', but rather that it is not the state's job either to identify and promote a particular comprehensive truth, or to oppose it.

ACCOMMODATION

More practically still, how can human rights courts begin to develop techniques to help stimulate a genuine dialogue that encourages secularity and furthers a pluralistic vision of the public space? The ECtHR has been consistently misguided in not developing the tool of proportionality in such a way as to enable it to deal with these claims. In this respect, the German, Canadian, and South African courts provide a considerably better model of how to address difficult religious litigation cases, not least because they have identified human dignity as underpinning the claims of *both* those who are seeking to restrict religious practices, *and* those who are seeking to manifest their religious beliefs. To repeat what Justice Sachs said in *Christian Education South Africa*, 'The right to believe or not to believe, and to act or not to act according to his or her beliefs or non-beliefs, is one of the key ingredients of any person's dignity ... [R]eligious belief has the capacity to awake concepts of self-worth and human dignity which form the cornerstone of human rights.' This use of 'dignity' thus enables a degree of commensurability to be identified between the values to be balanced in situations where there is an apparent clash of the rights protected. The solution adopted should be that which is most compatible with advancing 'human dignity'. Neither side of the debate is ruled out of court, there are no 'outlaws', and respectful attention is given to the claims of both parties.

The Canadian and South African courts approach the interpretation of rights and interests in ways that attempt to create the maximum space for rights by, seemly paradoxically, requiring both sides in the dispute not to push their rights or interests to the limit. This way of thinking about the role of rights in true dialogue has been taken up, for example, by Judge Sachs in the South African Constitutional Court, when he sought to inject aspects of mediation into resolving rights disputes, because it was vital for all those involved in the dispute to recognize that they were involved in a community with each other. It is akin, also, to what the German Constitutional Court has termed the principle of 'practical concordance'. 'This conflict among various bearers of a fundamental right guaranteed without reservation, and between that fundamental right and other constitutionally protected objects', the Court held in the famous *Classroom Crucifix* case, 'is to be resolved on the principle of practical concordance, which requires that no one of the conflicting legal positions be preferred and maximally asserted, but all given as protective as possible an arrangement'. Both rights carry significant weight. They should therefore both be protected to the greatest extent possible, and this requires that each be accommodated to the greatest extent possible by the other. Only by each side 'backing off' from making claims that assert its interests to the limit, can this be accomplished.

RELATIONALITY

As this shows, what is at stake, often, is the importance of relationality. What are the implications for practical decision making if relationality were to be taken more seriously? One effect is likely to be that previous justifications of rights based in a narrow conception of autonomy may have to be rethought more widely. Sedmak urges us to emphasize much more the importance of relationality rather than autonomy in our understanding of human rights, with important implications for some specific rights. Socio-economic rights would be rethought, for example, as protecting *relational* aspects of human flourishing to maximize the recognition and protection of our dignity, rather than as protecting the exercise of autonomy. This is not to say that a relational approach is incapable of coexisting with all understandings of autonomy. A focus on autonomy does not have to adopt a conception of the individual as ruggedly individualistic. Indeed, one can argue that autonomy often results from the existence of certain kinds of supportive relationships.

A renewed emphasis on relationality would also be useful in other contexts, not least in understanding the *telos* of freedom of religion. For Rivers, underestimating the importance of relationality is central to the weakness of current conceptions of dignity as a legal foundation for freedom of religion. Harrison takes this further, arguing that a personalist understanding of the person points towards a stronger associational account of religious liberty. It might also help us appreciate different ways of reinterpreting famous instances in which dignity is perceived as unduly antagonistic to autonomy interests, where dignity sometimes appears as a restriction on liberty for paternalistic reasons (for example, prohibiting dwarf-throwing). On closer inspection, these may appear to be more about restricting the perceived adverse impact of a social practice on *other* people who belong to a category that is subject to discrimination or low status. The prohibition based on dignity is to protect that larger category, rather than paternalistically trying to tell the individual whose actions are restricted that the society knows best for them.

WHAT DIFFERENCE WOULD IT MAKE?

What difference would an approach based on pluralism, secularity, accommodation, and relationality make to the way in which religious litigation would be adjudicated? Several judgments in which my preferred approach plays a central role illustrate how this could work in practice. In *Multani*, for example, the Canadian Supreme Court struck down the order of a Quebec school authority that had prohibited a Sikh child from wearing a kirpan to school; the Court considered that the 'minimal impairment' element of proportionality required the state to satisfy the court on the basis of evidence that a reasonable accommodation of the religious practice could not be achieved. In *Christian Education South Africa*, Sachs J (giving the judgment of the Court) stated:

> The underlying problem in any open and democratic society based on human dignity, equality and freedom in which conscientious and religious freedom has to be regarded with appropriate seriousness, is how far such democracy can and must go in allowing members of religious communities to define for themselves which laws they will obey and which not. Such a society can cohere only if all its participants accept that certain basic norms and standards are binding. Accordingly, believers cannot claim an automatic right to be exempted by their beliefs from the laws of the land. *At the same time, the state should, wherever reasonably possible, seek to avoid putting believers to extremely painful and intensely burdensome choices of either being true to their faith or else respectful of the law.*

Significantly, it was this approach that influenced Justice Sachs, in *Minister of Home Affairs* v. *Fourie*, the South African Constitutional Court's decision upholding a claim that the Constitution obliged the state to provide a means of recognizing same-sex unions. He required that state registrars who objected on religious grounds should be permitted not to be involved in granting such recognition. Justice Sachs, giving the judgment of the Court, stated: 'The principle of reasonable accommodation could be applied by the state to ensure that civil marriage officers who had sincere religious objections to officiating at same-sex marriages would not themselves be obliged to do so if this resulted in a violation of their conscience.'

In *Ladele*-type situations, such an approach seems particularly apposite, where the tension is between the right to non-discrimination on grounds of religion and the right to non-discrimination on grounds of sexual orientation, and there is no principled basis for deciding which should have priority. There was no indication in the national Court's decision, nor in the ECtHR, why one is less worthy of the strongest protection than the other. Indeed, the local authority's own policy, Dignity for All, under which the domestic court considered that the local authority was acting, protected employees from both religious discrimination and discrimination on grounds of sexual orientation, without ranking them in importance.

The appropriate solution would have been for the national authorities to consider whether Ms Ladele's conscientious objection could be reasonably accommodated, along the lines suggested by Justice Sachs. Applying an accommodationist approach, properly understood, the Court could have sought to preserve to the maximum extent possible *both* the right to sexual orientation equality *and* the right to religious equality, where they are or may be in conflict. And had this approach been adopted, the *Ladele* case itself might have seemed a relatively easy one, because in that case, there was in fact no conflict between the rights of Ms Ladele and those of actual same-sex couples seeking civil partnerships. Her conscientious objection could have been accommodated without any adverse effects on actual same-sex couples. Ms Ladele was disciplined not to protect any actual same-sex couple (whose rights were not, therefore, impeded in practice) but to use the disciplining of a public servant to 'send a message' to the wider community. In such a situation, the court ought to have held that there could be no proportionate justification for refusing to accommodate her conscientious objection.

SCEPTICISM ABOUT PLURALISM?

It would be surprising if these suggestions did not attract significant pushback. In particular, I suspect, claiming the role for pluralism that I do is likely to give rise to considerable scepticism. There are several reasons. We have seen that the language of 'pluralism' is often associated with a political strategy that aims to enable those who fundamentally disagree to live together, while continuing to disagree. The pluralism that results is one which is expected to be permanent, or at least long term—we don't expect ever to agree about abortion, or euthanasia, and so we say that the best solution is political pluralism. Human rights law, however, might be said to aim at *changing* perceptions and beliefs rather than simply accommodating them; human rights courts should not be content simply with reflecting the *status quo* of an existing deeply divided political culture. It should aim, rather, to bring about a changed political culture in which certain principles, assumptions, and beliefs are no longer accepted or acceptable. A pluralistic approach, it will be said, is uncertain at best, and at worst an approach that cuts the feet from under the emancipatory, change-driven, and historically based aims of current human rights law.

Were that to be the case, I admit that I would be worried, but I am not. To explain why, it is necessary to point to a problem within certain human rights approaches more generally. Crudely (and I admit that it is a crude description), some approaches to human rights are built on a view that in any dispute invoking human rights law, it is possible to identify which of the two parties comes from a group that is most subordinated, or is the greater victim, or is the most vulnerable, and that where the action of the other leads to that person becoming more subordinated, more vulnerable, more of a victim, human rights law should step in and add its weight to that vulnerable person's claim.

The problem is that, increasingly, particularly where there is a human rights claim on both side of the dispute, it is difficult easily to identify the most disadvantaged, or the most subordinated. So, in a *Ladele*-type, on one level of analysis, we might say that it is clear that Christians in England are much less subordinated than those who are gay, and therefore that a marriage registrar refusing to marry homosexuals should lose. But the reality is, of course, a lot more complex than that. Ms Ladele was a Christian, but she was also black, a member of a small Evangelical Church, working in Islington Council, which is among the most LGBT-friendly local authorities in London, a city that is among the most secular in the world. In this context, who is the most subordinated? So, too, in the *Ashers* case, who is more isolated and vulnerable, Mr Lee, the gay man who wanted to buy the cake with the pro-same-sex marriage message on it, or the bakers? To import such a test into human rights adjudication smacks of desperation or despair at the possibility of legal decision making that is other than emotion camouflaged as judgement. Surely, we can do better than that.

9

HOW SHOULD RELIGIONS APPROACH HUMAN RIGHTS?

I suggested in the previous chapter that a worthy aim would be to identify strategies that enable a genuine dialogue to take place over the most contested questions in human rights. I suggested that this has important implications for how human rights should be practised in the *courts*. The central question that this chapter addresses is whether *organized religion* is capable of engaging in true dialogue, and what changes in approach from religious actors would help to secure such a dialogue.

THE POSSIBILITY OF A DIALOGUE WITH RELIGION? THE CASE OF POPE BENEDICT

Nigel Biggar sees a 'very deeply rooted' view that 'religious discourse [in the public sphere] is uniquely menacing because it is uniquely characterized by dogmatic certainty and authoritarian appeal, and is therefore "unreasonable" in the sense of being incapable of the discursive give-and-take requisite to secular peace'. Yet he goes on to argue that the contrary is in fact true: 'The fact that religious arguments are informed by certain authorities does not mean', as Biggar puts it, 'that these proponents are incapable of deliberating, reasonably and critically, with those who differ from them'.

Indeed, religious leaders often say they want a genuine dialogue with secular society, including human rights advocates. It was a constant theme in Pope Benedict's speeches that dialogue is seen as positive. The Pope referred, approvingly, at the Collège des Bernardins, to 'dialogue between Christian Wisdom and the cultural, intellectual, and artistic currents of contemporary society'. At the United Nations, he acknowledged that '[d]ialogue

Litigating Religions: An Essay on Human Rights, Courts, and Beliefs. Christopher McCrudden. Published 2018 by Oxford University Press.

should be recognized as the means by which the various components of society can articulate their point of view and build consensus around the truth concerning particular values or goals'. Above all, at Westminster Hall, he emphasized the need for dialogue as his central message. '[T]he world of reason and the world of faith—the world of secular rationality and the world of religious belief—need one another and should not be afraid to enter into a profound and ongoing dialogue, for the good of our civilization'. His closing lines, indeed, return to this theme: 'I would invite all of you, therefore, within your respective spheres of influence, to seek ways of promoting and encouraging dialogue between faith and reason at every level of national life.'

If a dialogue is to be encouraged, religious authorities need to have an understanding of the internal legal viewpoint just as much as lawyers and judges need to have an understanding of the internal religious point of view. Yet some of what Benedict said seems problematic in this respect. Benedict rightly pointed out that human rights is not 'exclusively' or 'purely' the creation of law. In the United Nations speech, however, he went further, arguing that '[e]xperience shows that legality often prevails over justice when the insistence upon rights makes them appear as the exclusive result of legislative enactments or normative decisions taken by the various agencies of those in power. When presented purely in terms of legality, rights risk becoming weak propositions divorced from the ethical and rational dimension which is their foundation and their goal.' On one reading, this is simply a call for human rights not to be seen as the exclusive preserve of lawyers, and (perhaps especially for lawyers) that is a necessary corrective. Indeed, it is entirely consistent with what was suggested in Chapter 7's reconstruction of human rights theory.

A more complex reading of Benedict is possible, however, which is interesting, but jurisprudentially challenging. What, for example, is the message that is here sent to judges interpreting human rights standards? If, as I suspect, the message that Benedict intended to send is that human rights should be interpreted in light of their underlying normative underpinnings, this again is consistent with my earlier argument and is relatively uncontroversial, opening up the complex issue of how far legal interpretation is (and should be) relatively autonomous, from politics and from religious belief.

There are indications in other speeches that a more radical approach, denying the autonomy of judicial interpretation, was finding its way into Benedict's speeches before he retired. In one particularly notable criticism of the decision of the Inter-American Court of Human Rights regarding *in vitro* fertilization, Benedict described the Court as 'arbitrarily' redefining 'the moment of conception' and weakening 'the defence of unborn life', which he regarded as a 'source of concern'. How should we read this criticism, in particular his description of the Court as having acted 'arbitrarily'? This is, of course, a very significant charge to level at a court and one that I assume was not made lightly. For Benedict to attack a major respected international human rights court for acting 'arbitrarily' appears to strike at the legitimacy of the Court more generally.

It is now commonplace for politicians in many countries to criticize judges for the human rights decisions they make, usually for populist advantage, but the precise basis of the criticism is seldom very clear; nor is it here. Is Benedict's criticism of the Court that the judges made the 'wrong' decision? And, if so, was the decision wrong legally, or wrong morally? If wrong legally, then (with the deepest respect), it is unclear why Benedict considers himself qualified to make that judgement. If, as is surely more likely, he means to say that it is wrong morally, then it is unclear what he would have wanted the judges to do. Should the judges have simply ignored the legal imperatives and imposed a moral judgement? That, surely, cannot have been Benedict's intention, given the very significant challenge this poses for the rule of law, which prizes the idea that judges should act according to law. We are rightly concerned when judges act outside the law. The Inter-American Court of Human Rights is a court of *law*, not of *morals*, after all. If the sought-for dialogue is to include judges who interpret human rights law, and human rights lawyers more generally, as I hope it does, a more carefully nuanced approach to the relationship between law and morals is required.

But there is a deeper problem, I suggest. It is clear that Pope Benedict considered that there is a fundamental contribution that religion can bring to public reason. The relationship between faith and reason that he called for is not without considerable subtlety. He clearly did not envisage the Church as simply representing 'faith', and secular society representing 'reason'. Dialogue was essential for Benedict partly because of the sheer complexity of many of the issues faced by humanity. In an important statement to the Bundestag, he appears to acknowledge the difficulty of moving from an understanding of human rights based on the fundamental dignity of the human person to the identification of the precise practical implications of this insight. He asks, straightforwardly, 'how do we recognize what is right?', and answers thoughtfully and modestly that 'in terms of the underlying anthropological issues, what is right and may be given the force of law is in no way simply self-evident today. The question of how to recognize what is truly right and thus to serve justice when framing laws has never been simple, and today in view of the vast extent of our knowledge and our capacity, it has become still harder.'

When we read this together with his Westminster speech, the role of the Church he envisaged does not appear to be one of prescribing detailed solutions to fiendishly difficult practical problems, but one of helping people to orient their decisions correctly. '[T]he role of religion in political debate', he says, 'is not so much to supply ... norms, as if they could not be known by non-believers—still less to propose concrete political solutions, which would lie altogether outside the competence of religion—but rather to help purify and shed light upon the application of reason to the discovery of objective moral principles'.

However, is a 'profound and ongoing dialogue' *really* possible with the Catholic Church on human rights? Despite the evident desire for such a dialogue, and the significant degree of overlapping consensus, Benedict's speeches may be seen as offering an engagement with secular human rights only on terms that may mean that no genuine dialogue is possible, except with others of faith. Benedict attached importance to the difficulty of deciding what is right, and how the Church should not rush to 'concrete political solutions', but having apparently freed us to exercise our reason, we are then confronted with a set of very specific norms that Benedict found to be inherent in natural law, objectively valid, and, as David Kirchhoffer observes, 'more importantly, non-negotiable'.

There is little apparent recognition of the ambiguity in the understanding of dialogue, and this risks misleading people of good will outside the Church. One example must suffice to illustrate the general point, involving the profoundly tragic position that women contemplating abortions face. What would a dialogue between religion and human rights look like? In a speech in January 2013, Benedict noted 'with dismay' how in various countries, 'even those of Christian tradition', 'efforts are made to introduce or expand legislation which decriminalizes abortion'. The reason for this dismay, he said, is because direct abortion is 'gravely contrary to the moral law'. He appeared to link this directly with a concern 'lest the law unjustly alter the balance between the right to life of the mother and that of the unborn child, a right belonging equally to both'.

The issue I raise here is not whether abortion is morally wrong. Assuming it is, what is the role of the state? What is troubling in Benedict's remarks was the specificity of the political function that law was expected to play in regulating abortion. There are two particularly problematic assumptions. First, the implication that state law should generally prohibit that which is 'gravely contrary to the moral law' gives little or no attention to the problems such an approach generates in a pluralistic democracy where what is the morally right course of action is essentially contested. Second, the implication that the best way of balancing the right to life of the mother and that of the unborn child is by *criminalizing* abortion assumes a particular role for the criminal law. Several problems arise. If abortion is criminalized, how does this 'balance' the two rights? Does it not simply prioritize the right of the unborn child over that of the mother in all circumstances? And even if the primary concern is with the right to life of the unborn child, why is criminalization necessarily the best way to achieve this aim? What if there is empirical information that shows that the destruction of unborn life is *less* likely if abortion is decriminalized? Or is the law in this area to be seen as primarily expressive rather than instrumental? In short, the strong preference for criminalization of abortion, apparently in all circumstances, generates exactly the sort of 'concrete political solutions', which

Pope Benedict said 'would lie altogether outside the competence of religion'.

It seems doubtful that a black-and-white rule that abortion should be criminalized in all circumstances encourages 'the application of reason' either by the legislature, or, more importantly, by the woman herself. Criminalization, rather, involves the application of state coercion on the basis of a simple rule of thumb: it precisely *prevents* the application of reason in highly complex, individual moral contexts; it substitutes brute force, applied by the state. How is the absoluteness of the norm reconcilable with the highly nuanced, complex understanding of the human that human dignity requires?

What is the appropriate balance to be struck between positive and negative freedom, between the individual and community, and between subjectivity and objectivity, in arriving at a rich analysis of the concept of human dignity? Too often it can appear that Benedict was only willing to see human dignity from an objective–communitarian standpoint, in part because he perceived the secular world as only conceiving it from a subjective–individualistic standpoint. In correctly identifying the over-identification of human dignity with autonomy, he risked sliding too far towards the other extreme, where interiority, negative freedom, subjectivity, and individuality were substantially driven away from an understanding of what dignity involves.

Part of the problem the Church faces in engaging in a dialogue with secular human rights is that these specific dogmatic norms appear to be statements of objective truth which are not open to the type of dialogue that appears to be offered elsewhere. Experience teaches us that it is when the Church moves from 'purifying and shedding light on the application of reason to the discovery of objective moral principles' to 'proposing concrete political solutions', that it is most likely to run up against competing secular human rights approaches. On the one hand, we see clearly Benedict's enthusiasm for dialogue, for an engagement between faith and reason. On the other hand, we see many of the areas in which engagement might take place apparently closed off from questioning, often on the basis of an unexamined understanding of tradition. How can this apparent paradox be resolved? It is time to consider what we mean by 'tradition'.

TRADITION

There are two competing conceptions of tradition in evidence, and I suggest that, at the centre of the debate between Catholics and human rights advocates, we find not just a debate over the nature of human rights, but also over the nature of tradition itself, a debate as to which of these two competing conceptions of tradition to adopt.

Edward Shils proposed one sociological definition of the concept in 1981. For Shils, a tradition was that which is 'transmitted or handed down from the past to the present'. One way of viewing a tradition, drawing on this definition, is that it is a reflection of the past, with a substantive, unchanging content. There are additional aspects of this approach to tradition that often seem to be associated with this definition. Tradition is seen as irrational, because it is viewed as clinging to the past, simply because it is the past. The past that is to be preserved by tradition is usually understood as primarily concerned with substantive content: traditional marriage, sexual constancy, etc. As a result, it is frequently seen as better understood as a descriptive rather than as a normative category. Combined together, we can call this the 'orthodox' understanding of the idea of tradition.

Drawing on recent sociological and philosophical scholarship, I want to suggest, however, that there is now a significant challenge to this orthodox view of tradition, and that this different way of thinking about tradition better enables a genuine dialogue to take place. There are four significant challenges to the orthodox concept that this alternative understanding presents. Out of these negative challenges to orthodoxy, an alternative conception emerges.

First, tradition should be seen less as a reflection of the past than as a way of understanding the present. Richard Bauman, for example, has described how anthropological inquiry has moved to view tradition and related notions 'as symbolic, interpretive constructions in and of the present through the invocation of links to a meaningful past'. So too, Langlois considers that sociology is less concerned to view contemporary uses of tradition as embedded in an actual past and 'now integrates tradition into analyses of ongoing social change. In recent works, tradition is used to define a type of society (be it theoretical or empirical).'

Second, tradition is seen not as static but as often in flux. Traditions change over time. For Langlois, '[t]radition is a transmitted heritage which survives and orients contemporary actions, but this heritage is often transformed'. Traditions often have, as Patrick Glenn has pointed out in his study of 'legal traditions', a relatively stable core but no fixed boundaries. Major traditions are often complex, incorporating traditions within traditions. They usually contain a mechanism by which aspects of the tradition are interpreted. They also often incorporate a conception of change and a method by which change comes about, sometimes through selective incorporation of external ideas. There is often a degree of tension between what might be thought of as the doctrinal, or idealized, understanding of the tradition, and the social practice of those in the tradition. This tension also requires to be managed, not infrequently resulting in change in the social practice or, perhaps more frequently, in the way in which the doctrine is articulated.

Third, tradition should be seen as an example of rationality rather than irrationality. To act on the basis of 'tradition' has been seen as irrational, a criticism that was characteristic of Enlightenment thought. However, Raymond Boudon has advanced a contrary argument. He suggests that there are five different kinds of rationality: utilitarian rationality, teleological rationality, axiological rationality, traditional rationality, and cognitive rationality. As Langlois, explains: 'All of these types of rationality describe the good reasons why the actor is driven to act in a certain way. ... Custom and habit can also incite individuals to act in a certain way. Therefore, when one speaks of traditional rationality—"it has always been that way"—he is speaking of one type of rationality among others.'

Fourth, in this alternative understanding, tradition is seen as less concerned with the substantive content of the tradition, and more with the act of transmission of the tradition. Terrence Tilley distinguishes between two different elements in 'tradition': the act of transmission (in Latin, *traditio*), and the content handed down (in Latin, *tradita*). Important aspects of the complex normativity of tradition come more clearly into view when *tradita* and *traditio* are distinguished. Both conservative supporters and liberal critics consider tradition largely in the form of the *tradita*, missing the critical importance of the process of transmission as itself having normative value irrespective of the normativity of the *tradita*. Emphasizing *tradita* rather than *traditio* results in conservative support and liberal antagonism towards arguments based on traditional values because of an important dimension of the orthodox understanding of tradition discussed earlier, i.e. the extent to which tradition is static:

> to think primarily or exclusively of tradition as *tradita* is to suggest that what is important about tradition is what is handed down ... and the knowledge of what is handed down, not the practices by which these things are handed down. In this sense, if tradition is to maintain its identity, then it must keep the things it hands down the same. Hence, *tradita* often leads to the notion that tradition is an ossified given or hypostatized content.

Emphasizing *traditio*, on the other hand, does not necessarily bring with it this conservative baggage:

> What is missing from an understanding of tradition as a 'thing' to be 'handed down' in a supposedly 'uncorrupted' form is recognition of the malleable, inculturated and lived character of tradition as communicative and identity-shaping. Traditions shape beliefs, attitudes and actions of those persons who participate in them. In turn, individuals and communities reshape traditions in the very process of reception, transmission and enactment. The key insight for understanding tradition as a process that is necessarily open and responsive to context is the concept of practice.

There are, then, two radically different conceptions of tradition that emerge. The second conception, challenging the first, enables us to see more clearly why tradition is thought to provide a reason for action for those who share in that tradition, as well as why we should accord normative weight to it. Recently, philosophers have begun to explore the normativity of traditions 'that include norms of practice and behavior', and the work of Samuel Scheffler is particularly rich in this regard. Scheffler attempts to answer the question: 'What is it about traditions that leads people to treat them as reason giving?' He finds many 'different factors that may contribute to the perceived normative authority of a tradition'. His understanding of tradition is firmly within the second conception of tradition.

Traditions, he suggests, 'serve to establish and entrench certain social conventions' and in doing so 'facilitate social interaction and make it easier to achieve various individual and collective goals'. Traditions may take the form of 'collective habits' that 'enable us to settle without excessive and repetitive deliberation on courses of action that have, on balance, proved successful in the past'. We gain, he suggests, 'deliberative efficiency by relying relatively unreflectively on past practice as a defeasible guide to future conduct'. Traditions 'may be regarded as a repository of experience and of the kind of wisdom that comes from experience'. Subscribing to a tradition and acting in accordance with that tradition', Scheffler suggests, may 'be ways of expressing one's loyalty to others who adhered to the tradition and to whom such adherence was important'. We subscribe to the tradition in order to identify with, and keep close to, those in the past whom we respect; we respect them by following the traditions they followed.

Traditions not only embody values, they also provide for when those values come into effect and how those values are to be fulfilled. Establishing 'customs and conventions regarding the time and manner in which we fulfill' these values, reduces 'the indeterminacy of the norms and burdensomely discretionary character of the demands that they make of individuals'. Traditions may be followed because the tradition 'has played a formative role in a person's development' and the person 'may come to feel that what the tradition stands for is also what he or she stands for'. It comes 'to occupy a central place in the person's self-conception'. Acting on tradition 'may be experienced as a requirement of personal integrity'.

Scheffler's explanations, thus far, sound distinctly centred on the benefits that an individual gains from acting according to a tradition, but these do not exhaust Scheffler's account. Several of his explanations depend on the fact that traditional practices are, 'by their nature collective enterprises'. Thus, 'traditions provide important ways of enabling one to better deal with 'the vastness and impersonality of the universe and the precariousness and insignificance of our own place in it', by connecting ourselves to the past and the future: 'In acting in accordance with the traditional practice, the individual acts not only as she has acted in the past and as she will act in the future, but also as others acted before she was born and will act after she is dead.' The collective dimension is also critical in so far as these traditional practices 'are sustained not only by the allegiance of many adherents over long periods of time, but also by the adherents' mutual recognition of one another as collaborators in a shared enterprise'. This collective dimension reinforces this mutual connectedness. For Scheffler, a strong appeal of association with a tradition lies, significantly, in helping some to feel part of something that is bigger than themselves: 'One of its functions is to call attention to the limits of our egoism. We want to care about, and to value, things other than ourselves and our own flourishing.'

In particular, Scheffler sees the normativity of tradition in the *traditio* rather than the *tradita*. Not surprisingly, therefore, because he identifies the normativity in the *traditio*, Scheffler emphasizes the extent to which 'all traditions change over time and new generations always find ways to modify a traditional legacy in light of changing circumstances and outlooks'. It also explains why he considers that 'it would be a mistake to take an unduly dismissive attitude towards tradition as such or to view participation in a tradition as amounting to nothing more than a form of blind conservatism'.

This provides a strong reason why religious understandings of human rights, influenced by tradition, should be given respectful consideration, rather than dismissed out of hand. It provides a further reason for human rights courts to take more seriously religious viewpoints.

HUMAN RIGHTS CRITIQUE OF RELIGION

But this analysis of tradition also has important implications for organized religion. I'll again take the example of the Catholic Church to illustrate the point, although I believe that it may well apply to other organized religions. Conservatives within the Catholic Church, as well as secular liberal critics outside the Church, often overemphasize *tradita* rather than *traditio*, and it has been a theme in recent debates within the Church that this misperception needs to be corrected. In particular, there has been a re-examination of the extent to which understanding of human rights externally generated have offered, and can offer in the future, beneficial critiques of religion. Walsh argues that there are movements of the Spirit in the world outside Church and religion, and part of the way the Church has been called to account is by moral advances within secular thought, especially within the realm of rights and dignity. This secular language, he argues, has become an external moral challenge to Christianity. For Hanvey also, theology should develop its own self-critique. Vital to that self-critique are secular understandings of dignity. Theology needs a secular understanding as well as a theological understanding if it is to keep true to itself. Beattie goes further. One of the important developments of Vatican II, she suggests, was the acceptance that 'the full implications [of human dignity] cannot be known or affirmed apart from the concrete conditions of an historical epoch'. The Church's understanding of what human rights are required to promote human dignity is, therefore, subject to change, adaptation, and evolution.

Hollenbach illustrates well the elements of this more 'revisionist' approach. He argues that the interaction of reason and faith in shaping the Catholic understanding of dignity is a historical process, leading to notable revisions in the Catholic stance, and it will continue to do so. The Church is now and has always been deeply engaged with secular culture in developing its understanding of Church teaching, sometimes for the good and sometimes in unfortunate ways. Christianity started off in the first century AD, for example, with a very strong opposition to torture, but through the appropriation of Roman law came not only to endorse torture but to practise it. There are also examples, however, of progressive influences from secular culture that (sometimes grudgingly) led to significant changes in Church teaching, notably the acceptability of women in the workplace, and their right to be treated equally at work. So, too, the Church eventually reversed its position on torture, again influenced by developments in secular politics, and now declares that torture is one of the most fundamental violations of dignity of the person—an offence against God.

This change in teaching, in both cases, was influenced by the complex interaction between theology and secular culture that led to changing understandings of dignity and its implications. For Hollenbach, the moral is not that the Church should refuse to engage with culture, but that its conclusions as to what to understand from that culture should be modest, and in particular that the Church should be very careful about coming to premature absolutes in situations where human experience is still fast evolving. For Hollenbach, this approach echoes Thomas Aquinas's awareness of the implications of natural law: that the most fundamental principles of natural law are evident to all reasonable people and are changeless, but that the *applications* of these fundamental principles may not be at all self-evident and are changeable.

Church doctrine provides an opportunity for change, perhaps, informed by human rights. Benedict appears to acknowledge positive interactions between the Church and modernity at Regensburg: 'The positive aspects of modernity', he says, 'are to be acknowledged unreservedly: we are all grateful for the marvellous possibilities that it has opened up for mankind and for the progress in humanity that has been granted to us'. The Pontifical Council's *Compendium of the Social Doctrine of the Church* stresses that 'it must not be forgotten that the passing of time and the changing of social circumstances will require a constant updating . . . in order to interpret the new signs of the times'.

The Church needs an understanding of tradition, then, that is open to dialogue, and open to change. As Benedict said at Westminster: 'the world of reason and the world of faith—the world of secular rationality and the world of religious belief—need one another and should not be afraid to enter into a profound and ongoing dialogue, for the good of our civilization'. There is, in other words, a mutuality of need. A genuine conversation must allow the possibility of change on both sides; otherwise, it is simply an occasion for teaching, and not learning, and risks becoming discursive rather than dialogic. Benedict's warm embrace of the need for a dialogue between faith and reason is, therefore, a critical legacy of his papacy. It is strongly to be hoped that Benedict's commitment to dialogue will spread and become operationalized, and there are strong indications that his successor is similarly committed, but the mode of dialogue that should be promoted is one that is 'interested not only in handing on but also in generating, developing, or revising the truth' of religious traditions.

***

Vital to the self-critique that organized religions must engage in are secular understandings of dignity, but equally vital to the self-critique that secular human rights must engage in are understandings of dignity that are articulated by those with religious commitments. My suggestion is that the current litigation on human dignity and human rights is a place for both courts and religions to look, not for answers but for questions, and a forum in which to examine those questions further. The concept of human dignity invites openness to the posing of the question of what it is to be human in our public and communal discourse.

A dialogue with those who share that intuition, both those who are religious and those who are not, is all the more important because there is something irreducible about the human person that cannot be fully captured. This means that there is always a need for discussion, the likelihood of disagreement, and a certain under-determination. The very nature of what we are talking about—the human person—means that we should never presume to be able to specify dignity, or human rights, beyond contestation.

BIBLIOGRAPHICAL ESSAY

The purpose of this essay is to present an argument about the relationship between law, religion, and human rights that is accessible. I chose, therefore, not to weigh the text down with footnotes, either to reference quotations, or to refer to the extensive literature that has influenced my thinking. In this bibliographical essay, therefore, I aim to provide sufficient information for those interested to identify the sources I have quoted. The quotations and authors referred to in the previous chapters are identified in references (by the chapter and the page of the text in which the reference is found), followed by a citation in the form: 'author, date'. The full reference is contained in the bibliography, which will be found after these references. In preparing the lectures, and in revising them subsequently, I have drawn extensively on my previous academic work. Although the text of the essay is intended to be self-contained, readers will find in these chapters and articles more extensive discussion of many of the issues I raise in this essay, as noted below. In particular, readers will find in these sources references to the scholarly literature that I have drawn on. I am most grateful for permission to draw from and, in some cases, borrow extensively from these.

References

PREFACE

p. xi: 'stop thinking of human rights as trumps and begin thinking of them as a language that creates the basis for deliberation': Ignatieff, 2001, 95.

CHAPTER I

This chapter draws on McCrudden: 2015f; 2014c.

p. 3: 'the generalized "return" of religion to the public realm'; '[r]eligious deprivatization' (emphasis added): Haynes, 2012, 1.

pp. 8–9: JFS case: R(E) v. *Governing Body of JFS* [2009] UKSC 15 (UK Supreme Court).

pp. 9–10: Ladele case: Eweida v. *United Kingdom* (48420/10) (2013) 57 EHRR 8 (ECtHR).

pp. 10–11: Hobby Lobby case: Burwell v. *Hobby Lobby Stores Inc*, 573 US 22 (2014) (US Supreme Court).

pp. 11–12: Surayanda case: Surayanda v. *The Welsh Ministers* [2007] EWCA Civ 893 (Court of Appeal for England and Wales).

pp. 12–13: Hosanna-Tabor case: Hosanna-Tabor Evangelical Lutheran Church and School v. *Equal Employment Opportunity Commission*, 565 US 171 (2012) (US Supreme Court).

pp. 14–15: Obst case: Obst v. *Germany* (425/03) (ECtHR, 23 September 2010).

pp. 15–16: Schüth case: Schüth v. *Germany* (1620/03) (2011) 52 EHRR 32 (ECtHR).

p. 16: Şahin case: Şahin v. *Turkey* (44774/98) (2007) 44 EHRR 5 (ECtHR).

pp. 16–17: Lautsi case: Lautsi v. *Italy* (30814/06) (2012) 54 EHRR 3 (ECtHR).

pp. 17–18: Lawrence case: Lawrence v. *Texas*, 539 US 558 (2003) (US Supreme Court).

pp. 18–19: Obergefell case: Obergefell v. *Hodges*, 576 US ___ (2015) (US Supreme Court).

CHAPTER 2

This chapter draws on McCrudden: 2014c; 2018; 2012a; 2014a; 2015f; 2015c; 2008; 2015a; 2013b; 2011b.

p. 25: '[T]he Catholic Church's attitude towards human rights': Pontifical Commission, 'Iustitia et Pax' (Justice and Peace), *The Church and Human Rights*, Working Paper No. 1, 2nd edn, Vatican City, 2011, para. 18.

p. 25: '[I]nternationally accepted human rights standards are strongly supported': United States Catholic Bishops Pastoral Letter, *Economic Justice for All*: Catholic Social Teaching and the US Economy (1986), para. 80, http://www.usccb.org/upload/economic_justice_for_all.pdf

p. 27: 'It is . . . demanded by the common good', Pacem in Terris, para. 63.

p. 27: 'Rights to be free from economic deprivation': Shupack, 1993, 132–3.

p. 29: 'Essentialism is used in feminist writing': Blackburn, 2008.

p. 31: Human Rights Committee Resolutions on child marriages and forced marriages: HRC Resolution 24/23, Strengthening efforts to prevent and eliminate child, early and forced marriage: challenges, achievements, best practices and implementation gaps, A/HRC/24/2, 27 January 2014.

p. 31: 'a scattered left' 'a solid right': Lonergan, 1997, 252, 245.

p. 31: 'revisionist . . . anti-revisionist': John Langan, personal communication.

p. 32: New Natural Law: see, e.g., Bamforth and Richards, 2008. *New Natural Law and human dignity* ... Different authors within 'new natural law' place somewhat different emphases on the importance and centrality of 'dignity' to their enterprise. Contrast Finnis, 1998, 176–80, with Lee and George, 2008, 173.

p. 33: 'distinctive [Catholic] understanding of rights theory': Calo, 2011.

p. 34: 'The issue was first raised in 1999': Haynes, 2013, 21.

p. 35: 'extreme feministic views and homosexual attitudes': Russian Orthodox Church, UN Human Rights Council 7th Session Geneva, 18 March 2008 Panel discussion on Human Rights and Intercultural Dialogue (official translation provided by the Russian Orthodox Church).

p. 36: Lautsi case: *Lautsi* v. *Italy* (30814/06) (2012) 54 EHRR 3 (ECtHR).

p. 39: 'broad set of mutually reinforcing approaches or methodologies': Verovec and Wessendorf, 2010, 4.

p. 39: Decision by a school prohibiting a Sikh pupil wearing a turban to school rather than the authorized school uniform was held to amount to unlawful ethnic discrimination: Mandla v. *Dowell Lee* [1983] 2 AC 548.

p. 39: exemption for turban-wearing Sikhs: Motor-Cycle Crash Helmets (Religious Exemption) Act 1976, Section 2A (United Kingdom).

p. 39: 'British discourse on racialized minorities': Peach, 2005, 18.

p. 40: Grillo: Grillo, 2010, 57–8.

CHAPTER 3

This chapter draws on McCrudden: 2015b; 2015f.

p. 43: 'forms of organization characterized by voluntary, reciprocal, and horizontal patterns of communication and exchange': Keck and Sikkink, 1998, 8.

p. 43: 'private, voluntary, nonprofit, nonviolent groups with formal institutional character and aiming at some form of social change': Stachursky, 2013, 46.

p. 43: 'refers to the process by which social movements professionalize': Lang, 2013, 64.

p. 44: 'lengthy, but . . . not complicated': Lehr-Lehnardt, 2005, 35.

p. 45: 'a long-standing trend in the social and political science literature to overlook the role of religious actors in the public sphere': Berger, 2003, 17.

p. 45: 'formal organizations whose identity and mission are self-consciously derived': Berger, 2003, 16.

p. 45: 'now amounting to over 300 entities': Haynes, 2013, 4.

p. 46: 'need to connect to higher levels of decision-making': Berger, 2003, 20.

p. 46: 'Trying to exert such influence is especially problematic': Haynes, 2013, 6.

p. 48: Lawrence v. *Texas*: 539 US 558 (2003) (US Supreme Court).

p. 48: Hosanna Tabor v. *EEOC*: 565 US 171 (2012) (US Supreme Court).

p. 49: Steven Teles: Teles, 2008.

p. 50: Jivraj v. *Hashwani* [2011] UKSC 40 (UK Supreme Court).

p. 50: JFS: R(E) v. *Governing Body of JFS* [2009] UKSC 15 (UK Supreme Court).

p. 50: Christian Institute case: [2007] NIQB 66 [Northern Ireland High Court].

p. 51: Slovak Constitutional Court challenge: European Centre for Law and Justice, *Interest of Amici Curiae, Submitted to the Constitutional Court of the Slovak Republic*, PL. ÚS 12/01. The Court upheld the law as constitutional, PL ÚS 12/01, No. 1/2007.

p. 51: Swedish Supreme Court case; Romanian Constitutional Court case: see Bob, 2012, 86–89; 100–1.

p. 52: 'most global issues involve not just a single "progressive" movement promoting a cause, but also rivals fighting it': Bob, 2012, 2.

p. 52: 'cascade': the word is derived from Sikkink, 2011.

p. 53: Lautsi case: Lautsi v. *Italy* (30814/06) (2012) 54 EHRR 3 (ECtHR).

p. 53: A, B, C v. *Ireland*: (25579/05) (2011) 53 EHRR 13 (ECtHR).

p. 53: X v. *Austria*: (19010/07) (2013) 57 EHRR 14 (ECtHR).

p. 54: 'We're forced to do it': Bob, 2012, 83.

p. 54: Ladele/Eweida: (2013) 57 EHRR 8.

p. 54: 'remarkable opportunity': Alan E. Sears, *ADF Granted Right to Defend Four Crucial Cases*, www.alliancealert.org/2011

p. 55: Dudgeon: Dudgeon v. *United Kingdom*, Merits, Just Satisfaction, App. No. 7525/76, [1981] ECHR 5 (1982) 4 EHRR 149 (ECtHR).

p. 55: Inter-American Court of Human Rights: Atala Riffo v. *Chile*, Inter-Am. Ct. Hum. Rts, 24 February 2012 (Merits).

p. 55: Delhi High Court and Indian Supreme Court: Naz Foundation v. *Government of NCT of Delhi*, 2 July 2009 (High Court of Delhi); *Suresh Kumar Koushal and others* v. *Naz Foundation and others*, 11 December 2013 (Indian Supreme Court).

p. 56: Orozco v. *Attorney General of Belize*: for discussion, see Beirich, 2013; Ysaguirre, 2013.

p. 57: 'One of the characteristics of present-day denominations': Berger, 2003, 26.

p. 57: Haynes: Haynes, 2013, 11.

p. 57: Barnett and Stein: Barnett and Stein, 2012, 23.

p. 57: UN agreement on resolution condemning 'defamation of religions': see Haynes, 2013, 21–2.

pp. 57–58: Dispute over whether Canadian provincial government should establish Sharia tribunals: [Toronto] *Globe and Mail*, 26 October 2005.

p. 58: Nineteenth-century disputes in Scotland when the Church of Scotland split: Rodger, 2008.

p. 58: Long-running dispute between Orthodox and Reform Judaism over who can be a Jew: e.g. *R(E)* v. *Governing Body of JFS* [2009] UKSC 15.

CHAPTER 4

This chapter draws on McCrudden: 2018; 2014b.

p. 66: 'enables [us] to live in harmony': *R (Williamson)* v. *Secretary of State for Education and Employment* [2005] 2 AC 246 (UK House of Lords), at [15] (Lord Nicholls).

p. 66: 'period of harmony': *R (SB)* v. *Governors of Denbigh High School* [2007] 1 AC at 34 (UK House of Lords) (Lord Bingham). Other quotations in this paragraph at [80], per Lord Scott, at [79], per Lord Scott, and at [65], per Lord Hoffmann.

p. 67: 'The school's task is': R (SB) v. *Governors of Denbigh High School* [2007] 1 AC at 96 (Lady Hale).

p. 67: 'religious freedom is primarily a matter of individual conscience': Hasan and Chaush v. *Bulgaria* (2002) 34 EHRR 55 at [60] (ECtHR, emphasis added).

p. 68: 'religious communities traditionally and universally exist in the form of organised structures. They abide by rules which are often seen by followers as being of a divine origin': Hasan and Chaush v. *Bulgaria* (2002) 34 EHRR 55, at [62].

p. 68: 'religious freedom is primarily a matter of individual conscience': Hasan and Chaush v. *Bulgaria* (2002) 34 EHRR 55, at [60].

p. 68: 'the autonomous existence of religious communities': Hasan and Chaush v. *Bulgaria* (2002) 34 EHRR 55, at [61].

p. 69: 'it is also a precious asset for atheists, agnostics, sceptics and the unconcerned': Kokkinakis v. *Greece* (1993) 17 EHRR 397, at [31].

p. 69: 'the autonomous existence of religious communities': Hasan and Chaush v. *Bulgaria* (2002) 34 EHRR 55, at [61].

p. 69: 'the dynamics of cultural traditions': Gorzelik v. *Poland* (44158/98) (2005) 40 EHRR 4, at [92].

p. 69: 'Where the organization of the religious community is at issue': Hasan and Chaush v. *Bulgaria* (2002) 34 EHRR 55, at [62].

p. 70: Article 9 violated because of Bulgaria's 'interference with the internal organization of the Muslim community': Hasan and Chaush v. *Bulgaria* (2002) 34 EHRR 55, at [82].

p. 70: 'role of the authorities in such circumstances is not to remove the cause of the tension by eliminating pluralism': Serif v. *Greece* (38178/97) (2001) 31 EHRR 20, at [53].

p. 70: 'State measures favouring a particular leader': Metropolitan Church of Bessarabia v. *Moldova* (2002) 35 EHRR 13, para. 117.

p. 71: Thomas Jefferson's metaphor of a wall of separation between Church and State: Thomas Jefferson in a letter to the Danbury Baptists on 1 January 1802.

p. 75: Ladele case: *Eweida* v. *United Kingdom* (48420/10) (2013) 57 EHRR 8 (ECtHR).

p. 77: Romer v. *Evans*: 517 US 620, 646 (1996), quoting Jacobs, 1993, 724.

p. 78: 'race and lineage are congenital and unalterable traits over which an individual has no control and for which he should not receive neither blame nor reward': Developments in the Law, 1979, 1126–7.

p. 78: Eweida v. *British Airways:* [2010] EWCA Civ 80 (Court of Appeal for England and Wales (emphasis added).

p. 78: 'Intelligence, height, and strength are all immutable': Tribe, 1980, note 51.

p. 78: 'Discrimination against blacks': Balkin, 1997, 2365–6.

p. 80: Prohibition of some actuarial calculations based on gender of pension contributions under European Union law: Case 236/09, *Test-Achats*, judgment of 1 March 2011, [2011] 2 CMLR 38.

p. 80: Owen Fiss's 'group disadvantaging principle': Fiss, 1976.

p. 82: Recent British cases: e.g. *Eweida* v. *British Airways:* [2010] EWCA Civ 80 (Court of Appeal for England and Wales).

p. 82: 'within the ambit': e.g. *Thlimmenos* v. *Greece* (34369/97) (2001) 31 EHRR 411, at [42].

p. 83: Jehovah's Witnesses cases in the ECtHR: e.g. *Thlimmenos* v. *Greece* (34369/97) (2001) 31 EHRR 411.

p. 84: 'express a consensus about particular values of equality and the irrelevance of certain characteristics': Pitt, 2007, 213.

p. 86: Leyla Şahin case: *Şahin* v. *Turkey* (44774/98) (2007) 44 EHRR 5 (ECtHR).

CHAPTER 5

This chapter draws on McCrudden: 2014b; 2018; 2011b; 2011c; 2011a.

p. 88: Lautsi: Lautsi v. *Italy* (30814/06) (2012) 54 EHRR 3 (ECtHR).

p. 88: Hosanna-Tabor: Hosanna-Tabor Evangelical Lutheran Church and School v. *Equal Employment Opportunity Commission*, 565 US 171 (2012) (US Supreme Court).

p. 88: Ladele: Eweida v. *United Kingdom* (48420/10) (2013) 57 EHRR 8 (ECtHR).

p. 89: JFS case: *R(E)* v. *Governing Body of JFS* [2009] UKSC 15 (UK Supreme Court).

pp. 89–90: House of Lords 'but for' test: James v. *Eastleigh Borough Council* [1990] 2 AC 751 (UK House of Lords).

p. 92: Mandla v. *Dowell-Lee: Mandla* v. *Dowell Lee* [1983] 2 AC 548 (UK House of Lords).

p. 92: Keith Thomas: Thomas, 1971.

p. 93: H. L. A. Hart: Hart, 1961.

p. 93: Neil MacCormack: MacCormack, 1978, 292.

p. 94: Cases in Malaysia and Israel: HJH Halimatussaadiah Bte HJ Kamaruddin v. *Public Services Commission, Malaysia* [1994] 3 MLJ 61 (Supreme Court (Kuala Lumpur)); HC 72/62, *Rufeisen* v. *Minister of the Interior* PD 16 2428 (1962) (Justice Silberg).

p. 95: Supreme Court of Canada defines what constitutes a 'religion': Syndicat Northcrest v. *Amselem* (2004) SCC 47 (Supreme Court of Canada), from which the quotations in the rest of this paragraph are taken.

p. 96: Schüth: Schüth v. *Germany* (1620/03) (2011) 52 EHRR 32 (ECtHR).

p. 96: Obst: Obst v. *Germany* (425/03) (ECtHR, 23 September 2010).

p. 96: Surayanda: Surayanda case: Surayanda v. *The Welsh Ministers* [2007] EWCA Civ 893 (Court of Appeal for England and Wales).

p. 97: Preston Down Trust (PDT), Charity Commission: Charity Commission for England and Wales, Preston Down Trust: Application for Registration of the Preston Down Trust: Decision of the Commission, 3 January 2014.

p. 98: Grégoire Webber: Webber, 2009, 173.

p. 98: 'whatever their religious beliefs or cultural practices': Finnis, 2007, 6.

p. 98: 'to listen to others and a fairmindedness in deciding when accommodations to [one's] views should reasonably be made': Rawls, 2005, 217.

p. 99: 'Membership of a religion or faith normally indicates some degree of conscious affiliation with the religion or faith on the part of the member' JFS, at [44]. Lord Phillips.

p. 99: 'By choosing to classify themselves as NGOs': Berger, 2003, 35.

p. 100: 'that to be significant players in global public policy debates': Haynes, 2013, 6.

p. 100: 'Perspectives that are unique to a particular religion': Arsanjani, 2006, 173.

p. 100: Ashers Bakery case: Lee v. *McArthur and Ashers Bakery* [2016] NICA 39 (Northern Ireland Court of Appeal), currently on appeal to the UK Supreme Court.

CHAPTER 6

This chapter draws on McCrudden: 2015e; 2015a; 2012a; 2008; 2013b; 2015d; 2011b.

p. 103: 'unprepared to support a position so closely associated with Catholic religious teaching': Arsanjani, 2006, 173.

p. 103: 'made for life together in a universal community': Shupack, 1993, 129.

p. 103: David Hollenbach: Hollenbach, 1994.

p. 103: 'God gives man and woman an equal personal dignity': *The Catechism of the Catholic Church* (Continuum, 2000), ss. 2333–35, www.vatican.va/archive/ENG0015/_INDEX.HTM

p. 104: 'Men and women are equal as persons and complementary as male and female.' Congregation for the Doctrine of the Faith, 'Considerations Regarding Proposals to Give Legal Recognition to Unions between Homosexual Persons', at para. 3.

p. 104: I suggested in a previous article: McCrudden, 2008.

p. 104: 'that worth or value that people have simply because they are human': Sulmasy, 2008.

p. 107: Pope Benedict's theory of human rights: see McCrudden, 2015e, 165.

p. 107: James Hanvey: Hanvey, 2013.

p. 108: American Bishops' statement: United States Catholic Bishops Pastoral Letter, *Economic Justice for All*: Catholic Social Teaching and the US

Economy (1986), para. 80 http://www.usccb.org/upload/economic_justice_for_all.pdf

p. 108: 'Christian theologians': https://w2.vatican.va/content/benedict-xvi/en/speeches/2011/september/documents/hf_ben-xvi_spe_20110922_reichstag-berlin.html

p. 109: 'The Catholic tradition': https://w2.vatican.va/content/benedict-xvi/en/speeches/2010/september/documents/hf_ben-xvi_spe_20100917_societa-civile.html

p. 109: 'focuses on the reality of the person': Williams, 2005, 108.

p. 110: '[T]he Christian basis of any theory of human rights': Pontifical Council for Justice and Peace, *Towards Reforming the International Financial and Monetary Systems in the Context of Global Public Authority* (Vatican City 2011), para. 70.

p. 110: 'apply to everyone by virtue of the common origin of the person': Pope Benedict's speech at the United Nations, http://w2.vatican.va/content/benedict-xvi/en/speeches/2008/april/documents/hf_ben-xvi_spe_20080418_un-visit.html

p. 111: Sergio Dellavalle: Dellavalle, 2013.

p. 111: '[h]uman beings have dignity': Rosen, 2012, 31.

p. 112: Tollefsen: Tollefsen, 2013.

p. 112: Emily Jackson, cited in McCrudden, 2013b.

p. 112: '[t]he conclusion that intrinsic dignity': Sulmasy, 2008.

p. 113: 'human dignity means not only the individual dignity of the person': BVerfGE 45, 187, 229 (1977).

p. 113: Federal Administrative Court and 'peep shows': BVerwGE 64, 274 (1981).

p. 113: Dwarf-throwing cases: Conseil d'Etat (27 October 1995), req. nos. (136–727), Commune de Morsangsur-Orge, and 143–578 (Ville d-Aix-en-Provence); *Wackenheim* v. *France*, CCPR/C/75/D/854/1999: France, 26/07/2002, para. 7.4 (Human Rights Committee).

p. 113: Israeli censorship of films degrading to human dignity of women: Station Film Co. v. *Public Council for Film Censorship* (1994) 50 PD (5) 661.

p. 114: Justice Barak in Israeli Supreme Court's target killings case: Public Committee against Torture in Israel v. *Government of Israel*, HCJ 769/02 (Supreme Court of Israel Sitting as the High Court of Justice) [December 11 2005], para. 25.

p. 114: United States Supreme Court use of dignity in cases dealing with abortion, physician assisted suicide, and same-sex marriage case: Planned Parenthood of Southeastern Pennsylvania v. *Casey*, 505 US 833 (1992); *Washington* v. *Glucksberg*, 521 US 702 (1997); *Obergefell* v. *Hodges*, 576 US ___ (2015) (US Supreme Court).

p. 115: Jeremy Waldron: Waldron, 2012.

p. 115: Michael Rosen's book: Rosen, 2012.

p. 115: 'an expressive value demanding that people's behaviour, physical and verbal, convey a certain attitude to other people, namely an attitude of respect': Dan Cohen, 2000, 771.

p. 115: Tarun Khaitan: Khaitan, 2012.

p. 116: 'Ms Ladele's proper and genuine desire to have her religious views relating to marriage respected': *Ladele* v. *London Borough of Islington* [2009] EWCA Civ 1357 CA (Lord Neuberger MR), at [55].

p. 117: Khaitan on 'respect inflation': Khaitan, 2012, 15.

p. 117: 'what expresses contempt for human beings varies . . . between cultures and contexts': Rosen, 2012, 159.

p. 118: 'The right to believe or not to believe', *Christian Education South Africa* v. *Minister of Education* (CCT4/00) [2000] ZACC 11; 2000 (4) SA 757, Sachs, J., at [36].

p. 121: Ashers case: *Lee* v. *McArthur and Ashers Bakery* [2016] NICA 39 (Northern Ireland Court of Appeal), currently on appeal to the UK Supreme Court.

CHAPTER 7

This chapter draws on McCrudden: 2017; 2014c; 2013b; 2008.

p. 126: 'end of history': Fukuyama, 1992.

p. 128: sustained attempts by political philosophers to theorize about the meaning, scope and justification of human rights: In addition to those mentioned, the following have been particularly influential in my thinking: Luban, 2015; Besson, 2015; Raz, 2010a; Miller, 2015; Griffin, 2008; Raz, 2010b; Macklem, 2015; Tasioulas, 2012; Tasioulas, 2009; Habermas, 2010.

p. 129: Charles Beitz: Beitz, 2011.

p. 129: John Rawls: Rawls, 2001.

p. 130: Hans Joas: Joas, 2013.

p. 130: Charles Taylor: Taylor, 2007.

p. 130: John Milbank: Millbank, 2012.

p. 130: Nicholas Wolterstorff: Wolterstorff, 2010.

p. 130: John Rawls: Rawls, 2005.

p. 131: 'general justifying aim': the phrase is from Hart, 2008.

p. 131: Allen Buchanan: Buchanan, 2013.

p. 133: Liao and Etinson: Liao and Etinson, 2012, 327.

p. 133: Lea Ypi: Ypi, 2011.

p. 135: Richard Sennett: Sennett, 2012.

CHAPTER 8

This chapter draws on McCrudden: 2015c; 2015e; 2018; 2014b; 2013b.

p. 139: 'religious freedom is primarily a matter of individual conscience': *Hasan and Chaush* v. *Bulgaria* (2002) 34 EHRR 55 at [60] (ECtHR).

p. 139: 'it is also a precious asset for atheists, agnostics, sceptics and the unconcerned': *Kokkinakis* v. *Greece* (1993) 17 EHRR 397, at [31].

p. 139: 'the autonomous existence of religious communities': Hasan and Chaush v. *Bulgaria* (2002) 34 EHRR 55, at [61].

p. 140: Bradford Hinze: Hinze, 2006.

p. 141: 'comprehensive ideology': McConnell, 2001, 18.

p. 141: '[t]he "religion" of human rights and fundamental freedoms has replaced other religions and beliefs as the underpinning of social life in contemporary societies': Sacerdoti, 2002, 52.

p. 141: 'stop thinking of human rights as trumps and begin thinking of them as a language that creates the basis for deliberation': Ignatieff, 2001, 95.

p. 142: 'it is also a precious asset for atheists, agnostics, sceptics and the unconcerned': *Kokkinakis* v. *Greece* (1993) 17 EHRR 397, at [31].

p. 142: 'the dynamics of cultural traditions': Gorzelik v. *Poland* (44158/98) (2005) 40 EHRR 4, at [92].

p. 142: Scharffs on secularism and secularity: Scharffs, 2011.

p. 144: 'The right to believe or not to believe', Christian Education South Africa v. *Minister of Education* (CCT4/00) [2000] ZACC 11; 2000 (4) SA 757, Sachs, J., at [36].

p. 144: Sachs sought to inject aspects of mediation into resolving rights disputes: Port Elizabeth Municipality v. *Various Occupiers*, 2004 (12) BCLR 1268 (CC), Sachs J, at [39].

p. 144: Classroom Crucifix: Classroom Crucifix Case, BverfGE 93 1; 1 BvR 1087/91, 12 May 1987 (German Constitutional Court), C.II.3a.

p. 145: Sedmak: Sedmak, 2013.

p. 145: Rivers: Rivers, 2013.

p. 145: Harrison: Harrison, 2013.

p. 146: Multani: Multani v. *Marguerite-Bourgeoys*, 264 DLR (4th) 577, 2006 SCC 6, at paras. [51]–[53].

p. 146: Christian Education case: Christian Education South Africa v. *Minister of Education* (CCT4/00) [2000] ZACC 11; 2000 (4) SA 757, Sachs, J.

p. 146: Fourie case: Minister of Home Affairs v. *Fourie* (CCT 60/04) [2005] ZACC 19; 2006 (3) BCLR 355 (CC); 2006 (1) SA 524 (CC).

p. 147: Ladele case: Eweida v. *United Kingdom* (48420/10) (2013) 57 EHRR 8 (ECtHR).

p. 148: Ashers case: *Lee* v. *McArthur and Ashers Bakery* [2016] NICA 39 (Northern Ireland Court of Appeal), currently on appeal to the UK Supreme Court.

CHAPTER 9

This chapter draws on McCrudden: 2017; 2015e; 2015a; 2013b.

p. 150: Nigel Biggar: Biggar, 2009.

p. 150: 'dialogue between Christian Wisdom': https://w2.vatican.va/content/benedict-xvi/en/speeches/2008/september/documents/hf_ben-xvi_spe_20080912_parigi-cultura.html

pp. 150–151: '[d]ialogue should be recognized': http://w2.vatican.va/content/benedict-xvi/en/speeches/2008/april/documents/hf_ben-xvi_spe_20080418_un-visit.html

p. 151: 'world of reason and the world of faith': https://w2.vatican.va/content/benedict-xvi/en/speeches/2010/september/documents/hf_ben-xvi_spe_20100917_societa-civile.html

p. 152: other speeches: Address of His Holiness Pope Benedict XVI to the Members of the Diplomatic Corps Accredited to the Holy See, 7 January 2013, http://w2.vatican.va/content/benedict-xvi/en/speeches/2013/january/documents/hf_ben-xvi_spe_20130107_corpo-diplomatico.html

p. 152: decision of the Inter-American Court of Human Rights regarding in vitro fertilization: *Case of Artavia Murillo et al.* v. *Costa Rica*, Judgment of November 28, 2012, http://www.corteidh.or.cr/docs/casos/articulos/seriec_257_ing.pdf

p. 153: 'how do we recognize what is right?': https://w2.vatican.va/content/benedict-xvi/en/speeches/2011/september/documents/hf_ben-xvi_spe_20110922_reichstag-berlin.html

p. 154: David Kirchhoffer: Kirchhoffer, 2010.

p. 154: speech in January 2013: Address of His Holiness Pope Benedict XVI to the Members of the Diplomatic Corps Accredited to the Holy See, 7 January 2013, http://w2.vatican.va/content/benedict-xvi/en/speeches/2013/january/documents/hf_ben-xvi_spe_20130107_corpo-diplomatico.html

p. 156: Edward Shils: Shils, 1981, 12.

p. 156: Richard Bauman: Bauman, 2001.

p. 157: Langlois: Langlois, 2001.

p. 157: Glenn: Glenn, 2014.

p. 157: Raymond Boudon: Boudon, 1986; Boudon, 1992; Boudon, 2003; Boudon, 2007; Boudon and Bourricaud, 1986.

p. 157: Langlois: Langlois, 2001.

p. 157: Terrence Tilley: Tilley, 2000.

p. 158: Samuel Scheffler: Scheffler, 2012.

p. 161: Walsh: Walsh, 2013.

p. 161: Hanvey: Hanvey, 2013.

p. 161: Beattie: Beattie, 2013.

p. 161: Hollenbach: Hollenbach, 1979; 2013.

p. 162: Benedict at Regensburg: http://w2.vatican.va/content/benedict-xvi/en/speeches/2006/september/documents/hf_ben-xvi_spe_20060912_university-regensburg.html

p. 162: Pontifical Council's Compendium of the Social Doctrine of the Church: Compendium, para. 9, http://www.vatican.va/roman_curia/pontifical_councils/justpeace/documents/rc_pc_justpeace_doc_20060526_compendio-dott-soc_en.html

p. 162: Benedict at Westminster: https://w2.vatican.va/content/benedict-xvi/en/speeches/2010/september/documents/hf_ben-xvi_spe_20100917_societa-civile.html

BIBLIOGRAPHY

Arsanjani, Mahnoush H., 2006, 'Negotiating the UN Declaration on Human Cloning', 100(1) *American Journal of International Law* 164

Balkin, J. M., 1997, 'The Constitution of Status', 106 *Yale Law Journal*, 2313

Bamforth, Nicholas and Richards, David A. J., 2008, *Patriarchal Religion, Sexuality, and Gender: A Critique of New Natural Law* (Cambridge University Press)

Barnett, Michael and Stein, Janet Gross, 2012, *Sacred Aid: Faith and Humanitarianism* (Oxford University Press)

Bauman, R., 2001, 'Tradition, Anthropology of', *International Encyclopedia of the Social & Behavioral Sciences*, 15819

Beattie, Tina, 2013, 'The Vanishing Absolute and the Deconsecrated God: A Theological Reflection on Revelation, Law and Human Dignity', in Christopher McCrudden (ed.), *Understanding Human Dignity* (Proceedings of the British Academy, Oxford University Press)

Beirich, Heidi, 2013, *Dangerous Liaisons: The American Religious Right and the Criminalization of Homosexuality in Belize* (Southern Poverty Law Center)

Beitz, Charles, 2011, *The Idea of Human Rights* (Oxford University Press)

Berger, Julia, 2003, 'Religious Nongovernmental Organizations: An Exploratory Analysis', 14(1) *Voluntas: International Journal of Voluntary and Nonprofit Organizations* 15

Besson, Samantha, 2015, 'Human Rights and Constitutional Law', in Rowan Cruft, S. Matthew Liao, and Massimo Renzo (eds.), *Philosophical Foundations of Human Rights Law* (Oxford University Press)

Biggar, Nigel, 2009, 'Conclusion', in Nigel Biggar and Linda Hogan (eds.), *Religious Voices in Public Places* (Oxford University Press), 319–20

Blackburn, Simon, 2008, Entry on 'essentialism', in *The Oxford Dictionary of Philosophy* (Oxford University Press), http://www.oxfordreference.com/views/ENTRY.html?subview=Main&entry=t98.e1139

Bob, Clifford, 2012, *The Global Right Wing and the Clash of World Politics* (Cambridge University Press)

Boudon, R., 2007, *Essais sur la théorie générale de la rationalité* (PUF)

Boudon, R., 2003, *Raison, Bonnes raisons* (PUF)

Boudon, R., 1992, 'Action', in R Boudon (ed.), *Traité de sociologie* (PUF), 21–55

Boudon, R. and Bourricaud, F., 1986, *Dictionnaire critique de la sociologie*, 2nd edn (PUF)

Buchanan, Allen, 2013, *The Heart of Human Rights* (Oxford University Press)

Calo, Zachary R., 2011, 'Catholic Social Thought, Political Liberalism, and the Idea of Human Rights', 1 *Journal of Christian Legal Thought* 1–13

Dan-Cohen, Meir, 2000, 'Basic Values and the Victim's State of Mind', 88 *California Law Review* 770

Dellavalle, Sergio, 2013, 'From *Imago Dei* to Mutual Recognition: The Evolution of the Concept of Human Dignity in the Light of the Defence of Religious Freedom', in Christopher McCrudden (ed.), *Understanding Human Dignity* (Oxford University Press)

Developments in the Law: Equal Protection, 1979, *Harvard Law Review* 82: 1065

Finnis, John, 2007, 'On "Public Reason"', *Oxford Legal Studies Research Paper No.* 1/2007

Finnis, John, 1998, *Aquinas: Moral, Political and Legal Theory* (Oxford University Press)

Fiss, Owen M., 1976, 'Groups and the Equal Protection Clause', 5 *Philosophy and Public Affairs* 107

Fukuyama, Francis, 1992, *The End of History and the Last Man* (Free Press)

Glenn, Patrick, 2014, *Legal Traditions of the World* (Oxford University Press)

Grillo, Ralph, 2010, 'British and Others: From "Race" to "Faith"', in Steven Vertovec and Susanne Wessendorf (eds.), *The Multiculturalism Backlash: European Discourses, Policies and Practices* (Routledge)

Griffin, James, 2008, *On Human Rights* (Oxford University Press)

Habermas, Jürgen, 2010, 'The Concept of Human Dignity and the Realistic Utopia of Human Rights', 41(4) *Metaphilosophy* 464

Hanvey, James, 2013, 'Dignity, Person, Imago Trinitatis', in Christopher McCrudden (ed.), *Understanding Human Dignity* (Oxford University Press)

Harrison, Joel, 2013, '"A Communion in Good Living": Human Dignity and Religious Liberty beyond the Overlapping Consensus', in Christopher McCrudden (ed.), *Understanding Human Dignity* (Proceedings of the British Academy, Oxford University Press)

Hart, H. L. A., 2008, *Punishment and Responsibility: Essays in the Philosophy of Law*, 2nd edn (Oxford University Press)

Hart, H. L. A., 1961, *Concept of Law* (Oxford University Press)

Haynes, Jeffrey, 2013, 'Faith-based Organisations at the United Nations' (EUI Working Paper RSCAS 2013/70, Robert Schuman Centre for Advanced Studies)

Haynes, Jeffrey, 2012, *Religious Transnational Actors and Soft Power* (Routledge)

Hinze, Bradford, 2006, *Practices of Dialogue in the Roman Catholic Church: Aims and Obstacles, Lessons and Laments* (Continuum)

Hollenbach, David, 2013, 'Human Dignity: Experience and History, Practical Reason and Faith', in Christopher McCrudden (ed.), *Understanding Human Dignity* (Proceedings of the British Academy, Oxford University Press)

Hollenbach, David, 1994, 'A Communitarian Reconstruction of Human Rights: Contributions from Catholic Tradition', in R. Bruce Douglass and David Hollenbach (eds.), *Catholicism and Liberalism: Contributions to American Public Philosophy* (Cambridge University Press), 127–50

Hollenbach, David, 1979, *Claims in Conflict: Retrieving and Renewing the Catholic Human Rights Tradition* (Paulist Press)

Ignatieff, Michael, 2001, *Human Rights as Politics and Idolatry*, University Center for Human Values Series (Princeton University Press)

Jacobs, A. M., 1993, 'The Rhetorical Construction of Rights: The Case of the Gay Rights Movement, 1969–1991', 72 *Nebraska Law Review* 723

Joas, Hans, 2013, *The Sacredness of the Person* (Georgetown University Press)

Keck, Margaret and Sikkink, Kathryn, 1998, *Activists Beyond Borders: Advocacy Networks in International Politics* (Cornell University Press)

Khaitan, Tarun, 2012, 'Dignity as an Expressive Norm: Neither Vacuous Nor a Panacea', 32 *Oxford Journal of Legal Studies* 1

Kirchhoffer, David G., 2010, 'Benedict XVI, Human Dignity, and Absolute Moral Norms', 91(1035) *New Blackfriars* 586–608

Langlois, S., 2001, 'Traditions: Social', *International Encyclopedia of the Social & Behavioral Sciences* 15829

Lang, Sabine, 2013, *NGOs, Civil Society, and the Public Sphere* (Cambridge University Press)

Lee, Patrick and George, Robert, 2008, 'The Nature and Basis of Human Dignity', 21 *Ratio Juris* 173

Lehr-Lehnardt, Rana, 2005, 'NGO Legitimacy: Reassessing Democracy, Accountability and Transparency', Cornell Law School Inter-University Graduate Student Conference Papers, paper 6, 35 http://scholarship.law.cornell.edu/lps_clacp/6

Liao, S. Matthew and Etinson, Adam, 2012, 'Political and Naturalistic Conceptions of Human Rights: A False Polemic?', 9(3) *Journal of Moral Philosophy* 327

Lonergan, Bernard, 1967, 'Dimensions of Meaning', in Frederick E. Crowe (ed.), *Collection: Papers by Bernard Lonergan, S.J.* (Herder and Herder)

Luban, David, 2015, 'Human Rights Pragmatism and Human Dignity', in Rowan Cruft, S. Matthew Liao, and Massimo Renzo (eds.), *Philosophical Foundations of Human Rights Law* (Oxford University Press)

McConnell, Michael, 2001, 'Liberalism and People of Faith', in Michael McConnell et al. (eds.), *Christian Perspectives on Legal Thought* (Yale University Press)

MacCormack, Neil, 1978, *Legal Reasoning and Legal Theory* (Clarendon Press)

McCrudden, Christopher, 2018, 'Marriage Registrars, Same-Sex Relationships, and Religious Discrimination in the European Court of Human Rights', in Susanna Mancini and Michel Rosenfeld (eds.), *The Conscience Wars: Rethinking the Balance between Religion, Identity, and Equality* (Cambridge University Press) [forthcoming]

McCrudden, Christopher, 2017, 'A Comment on Patrick Macklem's *The Sovereignty of Human Rights*', *University of Toronto Law Journal* [forthcoming]

McCrudden, Christopher, 2015a, 'Human Rights, Southern Voices, and "Traditional Values" at the United Nations', in Upendra Baxi, Christopher McCrudden, and Abdul Paliwala (eds.), *Law's Global and Theoretical Contexts: Essays in Honour of William Twining* (Cambridge University Press), 38

McCrudden, Christopher, 2015b, 'Transnational Culture Wars', 13(2) *International Journal of Constitutional Law* 434

McCrudden, Christopher, 2015c, 'Human Rights Histories', 35 *Oxford Journal of Legal Studies* 179

McCrudden, Christopher, 2015d, 'Dignity and the Challenge to Liberty: Reading Andras Sajo's Constitutional Sentiments', in Renata Uitz (ed.), *Freedom and Its Enemies: The Tragedy of Liberty* (Issues in Constitutional Law, Boom Eleven International), 127

McCrudden, Christopher, 2015e, 'Benedict's Legacy: Human Rights, Human Dignity, and the Possibility of Dialogue', in Marta Cartabia and Andrea Simoncini (eds.), *Pope Benedict XVI's Legal Thought: A Dialogue on the Foundation of Law* (Cambridge University Press) 165

McCrudden, Christopher, 2015f, 'Faith-based Non-governmental Organizations in the Public Square', in Malcolm Evans, Peter Petkoff, and Julian Rivers (eds.), *The Changing Nature of Religious Rights under International Law* (Oxford University Press), 185

McCrudden, Christopher, 2014a, 'Reva Siegel and the Role of Religion in Constructing the Meaning of "Human Dignity"', in Hanoch Dagan, Shahar Lifshitz, and Yedidia Z. Stern (eds.), *Religion and the Discourse of Human Rights Discourse* (Israel Democracy Institute), 175

McCrudden, Christopher, 2014b, 'The Intersection of Religious Autonomy and Religious Symbols: Setting the Stage', in Liora Lazarus, Christopher McCrudden, and Nigel Bowles (eds.), *Reasoning Rights: Comparative Judicial Engagement* (Hart) (with Brett Scharffs), 207

McCrudden, Christopher, 2014c, 'The Pluralism of Human Rights Adjudication', in Liora Lazarus, Christopher McCrudden, and Nigel Bowles (eds.), *Reasoning Rights: Comparative Judicial Engagement* (Hart), 3–27

McCrudden, Christopher, 2013a, 'Dignity and Religion', in Robin Griffith-Jones (ed.), *Islam and English Law: Rights, Responsibilities and the Place of Shari'a* (Cambridge University Press), 94

McCrudden, Christopher, 2013b, 'In Pursuit of Human Dignity: An Introduction to Current Debates', in Christopher McCrudden (ed.),

Understanding Human Dignity (Proceedings of the British Academy, Oxford University Press), 1

McCrudden, Christopher, 2012a, 'Legal and Roman Catholic Conceptions of Human Rights', 1(1) *Oxford Journal of Law and Religion* 185

McCrudden, Christopher, 2011a, 'Catholicism, Human Rights and the Public Sphere', 5 *International Journal of Public Theology* 331

McCrudden, Christopher, 2011b, 'Post-Multiculturalism, Freedom of Religion, and Anti-discrimination Law: The *JFS* Case Considered', 9 *International Journal of Constitutional Law* 200

McCrudden, Christopher, 2011c, 'Religion, Human Rights, Equality and the Public Space', 13 *Ecclesiastical Law Journal* 26

McCrudden, Christopher, 2008, 'Human Dignity and Judicial Interpretation of Human Rights', 19(4) *European Journal of International Law* 655

Macklem, Patrick, 2015, *The Sovereignty of Human Rights* (Oxford University Press)

Milbank, John, 2012, 'Against Human Rights: Liberty in the Western Tradition', 1(1) *Oxford Journal of Law and Religion* 203

Miller, David, 2015, 'Raz on Human Rights', in Rowan Cruft, S. Matthew Liao, and Massimo Renzo (eds.), *Philosophical Foundations of Human Rights Law* (Oxford University Press)

Peach, Ceri, 2005, 'Muslims in the UK', in T. Abbas (ed.), *Muslim Britain: Communities Under Pressure* (Zed Books)

Pitt, Gwyneth, 2007, 'Religion or Belief: Aiming at the Right Target', in Helen Meenan (ed.), *Equality Law in an Enlarged European Union: Understanding the Article 13 Directives* (Cambridge University Press), 202

Rawls, John, 2005, *Political Liberalism* (Columbia University Press)

Rawls, John, 2001, *The Law of Peoples*, rev. edn (Harvard University Press)

Raz, Joseph, 2010a, 'Human Rights without Foundations', in Samantha Besson and John Tasioulas (eds.), *The Philosophy of International Law* (Oxford University Press), 321

Raz, Joseph, 2010b, 'Human Rights in the Emerging World Order', 1(1) *Transnational Legal Theory* 31

Rivers, Julian, 2013, 'Justifying Freedom of Religion: Does Dignity Help?', in Christopher McCrudden (ed.), *Understanding Human*

Dignity (Proceedings of the British Academy, Oxford University Press)

Rodger, Lord Rodger of Earlsferry, 2008, *The Courts, the Church and the Constitution: Aspects of the Disruption of 1842* (Edinburgh University Press)

Rosen, Michael, 2012, *Dignity: Its History and Meaning* (Harvard University Press)

Sacerdoti, Giorgio, 2002, 'The European Charter of Fundamental Rights: From a Nation-State Europe to a Citizens' Europe', 8 *Columbia Journal of European Law* 37

Scharffs, B. G., 2011, 'Four Views of the Citadel: The Consequential Distinction between Secularity and Secularism, Religion and Human Rights', 6 *Religion and Human Rights* 109–26

Scheffler, Samuel, 2012, 'The Normativity of Tradition', in Samuel Scheffler, *Equality and Tradition* (Oxford University Press)

Sedmak, Clemens, 2013, 'Human Dignity, Interiority, and Poverty', in Christopher McCrudden (ed.), *Understanding Human Dignity* (Proceedings of the British Academy, Oxford University Press)

Sennett, Richard, 2012, *Together: The Rituals, Pleasure and Politics of Cooperation* (Yale University Press)

Shils, Edward, 1981, *Tradition* (Faber)

Shupack, Martin, 1993, 'The Churches and Human Rights: Catholic and Protestant Human Rights Views as Reflected in Church Statements', 6 *Harvard Human Rights Journal* 127

Sikkink, Kathryn, 2011, *The Justice Cascade: How Human Rights Prosecutions are Changing World Politics* (Norton)

Stachursky, Benjamin, 2013, *The Promise and Perils of Transnationalization: NGO Activism and the Socialization of Women's Human Rights in Egypt and Iran* (Routledge)

Sulmasy, David P., 2008, *Dignity and Bioethics: History, Theory, and Selected Applications, in Human Dignity and Bioethics: Essays Commissioned by the President's Council on Bioethics* (President's Council on Bioethics), https://bioethicsarchive.georgetown.edu/pcbe/reports/human_dignity/chapter18.html

Tasioulas, John, 2012, 'Towards a Philosophy of Human Rights', 65(1) *Current Legal Problems* 1–30

Tasioulas, John, 2009, 'Are Human Rights Essentially Triggers for Intervention?', 4 *Philosophy Compass* 938

Taylor, Charles, 2007, *A Secular Age* (Harvard University Press)

Teles, Steven M., 2008, *The Rise of the Conservative Legal Movement: The Battle for Control of the Law* (Princeton University Press)

Thomas, Keith, 1971, *Religion and the Decline of Magic* (Weidenfeld & Nicholson)

Tilley, Terrence W., 2000, *Inventing Catholic Tradition* (Orbis)

Tollefsen, Christopher, 2013, 'The Dignity of Marriage', in Christopher McCrudden (ed.), *Understanding Human Dignity* (Proceedings of the British Academy, Oxford University Press)

Tribe, L. H., 1980, 'The Puzzling Persistence of Process-Based Constitutional Theories', 89 *Yale Law Journal* 1063

Verovec, Steven and Wessendorf, Susanne, 2010, 'Introduction: Assessing the Backlash against Multiculturalism in Europe', in Steven Vertovec and Susanne Wessendorf (eds.), *The Multiculturalism Backlash: European Discourses, Policies and Practices* (Routledge)

Waldron, Jeremy, 2012, *Dignity, Rank, and Rights* (Oxford University Press)

Walsh, David, 2013, 'Dignity as an Eschatological Concept', in Christopher McCrudden (ed.), *Understanding Human Dignity* (Proceedings of the British Academy, Oxford University Press)

Webber, Grégoire C. N., 2009, *The Negotiable Constitution: On the Limitation of Rights* (Cambridge University Press)

Williams, Thomas D., 2005, *Who Is My Neighbor?: Personalism and the Foundations of Human Rights* (Catholic University of America Press)

Wolterstorff, Nicholas, 2010, *Justice: Rights and Wrongs* (Princeton University Press)

Ypi, Lea, 2011, *Global Justice and Avant-Garde Political Agency* (Oxford University Press)

Ysaguirre, William G. 'Belize Action Not US Funded—Pastor Stirm', *Reporter Newspaper*, 5 August 2013

INDEX

INTRODUCTORY NOTE

References such as '128–9' indicate (not necessarily continuous) discussion of a topic across a range of pages. Wherever possible in the case of topics with many references, these have either been divided into sub-topics or only the most significant discussions of the topic are listed. Because the entire work is about 'religion', the use of this term (and certain others which occur constantly throughout the book) as an entry point has been restricted. Information will be found under the corresponding detailed topics.

The manufacturer's authorised representative in the EU for product safety is Oxford University Press España S.A. of el Parque Empresarial San Fernando de Henares, Avenida de Castilla, 2 – 28830 Madrid (www.oup.es/en or product.safety@oup.com). OUP España S.A. also acts as importer into Spain of products made by the manufacturer.

www.ingramcontent.com/pod-product-compliance
Lightning Source LLC
LaVergne TN
LVHW010320220926
848484LV00004BB/811
* 9 7 8 0 1 9 8 7 5 9 0 4 1 *